WHO FRAMED MY DOG?

As an artist I love all kinds of art. I have taken 30 dogs and 30 artists putting them together in a framed portrait. Each dog has a special name that is combined with the artist. In each portrait are symbols and elements reflecting the "style" of the artist. If you are not familiar with the artist, take a moment to look them up and look at their art. This will help you understand my vision and give you clues on how you might like to color the portrait. Dogs are my love and my passion Art tells a story and now you can color each one expressing your love for dogs and coloring.

Get your pens or pencils, relax and enjoy coloring these wonderful dogs!

Artist—Alisann Smookler

Art by Alisann

www.ArtbyAllisann.com

ADOPT**RESCUE**SPAY/NEUTER

NOTE: These pages are meant to take Crayons and Pencils, When using markers/pens I recommend using a Bleed Sheet Protector behind the page to protect the next page.

Coloring Title	Breed	Artist
Catgritt	Catahoula Hound	Rene Magritte
Dalsarley	Dalmatian	Victor Vasarely
Germanbraq	German Shepherd Pup	Georges Braque
Ladymastiff	Mastiff	Lady Pink
Wyethound	Red coon Hound	Andrew Wyeth
Chabox	Boxer	Marc Chagall
Pomvangogh	Pomeranian	Vincent Van Gogh
Chihualo	Chihuahua	Freda Kahlo
Rothdog	Bernese Mtn. Dog	Mark Rothko
Whippcasso	Whippet	Pablo Picasso
Corgiwell	Corgi	Norman Rockwell
Degaschnauzer	Mini Schnauzer	Edgar Degas
Winspaniel	Water Spaniel	Homer Winslow
Labtisse	Labrador	Henri Matisse
Cezpapillion	Papillion	Paul Cezanne
Georgia O'Spanieell	Cocker Spaniel	Georgia O'Keeffe
Gonet	Golden Retriever	Claude Monet
Warhound	Borzi Wolfhound	Andy Warhol
Husdinsky	Huskie	Wassily Kandinsky
Katxlish	English Spaniel	Alex Katx
Salvadordoxie	Dachshund	Salvador Dali
Klimut	Rhodesian Hound	Gustav Klimt
Rotharing	Rottweiler	Keith Haring
Koondog	Shiba Inu	Jeff Koons
Miroluki	Saluki	Joan Miro
Labhtenstein	Labrador	Roy Lichtenstein
Leonpollack	Leonberger	Jackson Pollack
Malaklee	Malamute	Paul Klee
PitbanC	Pitbull	Banksy
Maxspitz	German Spitz	Max Ernst

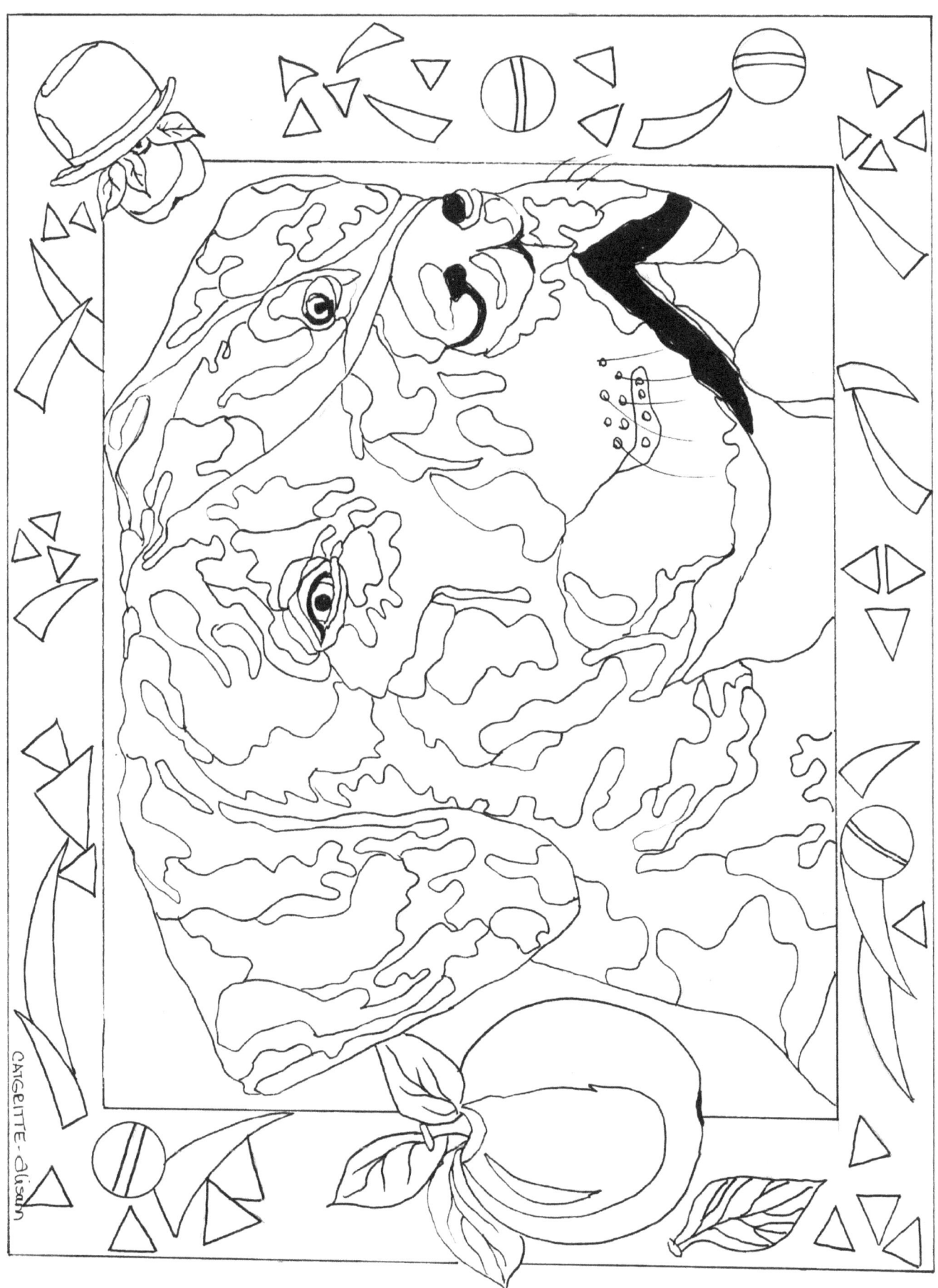

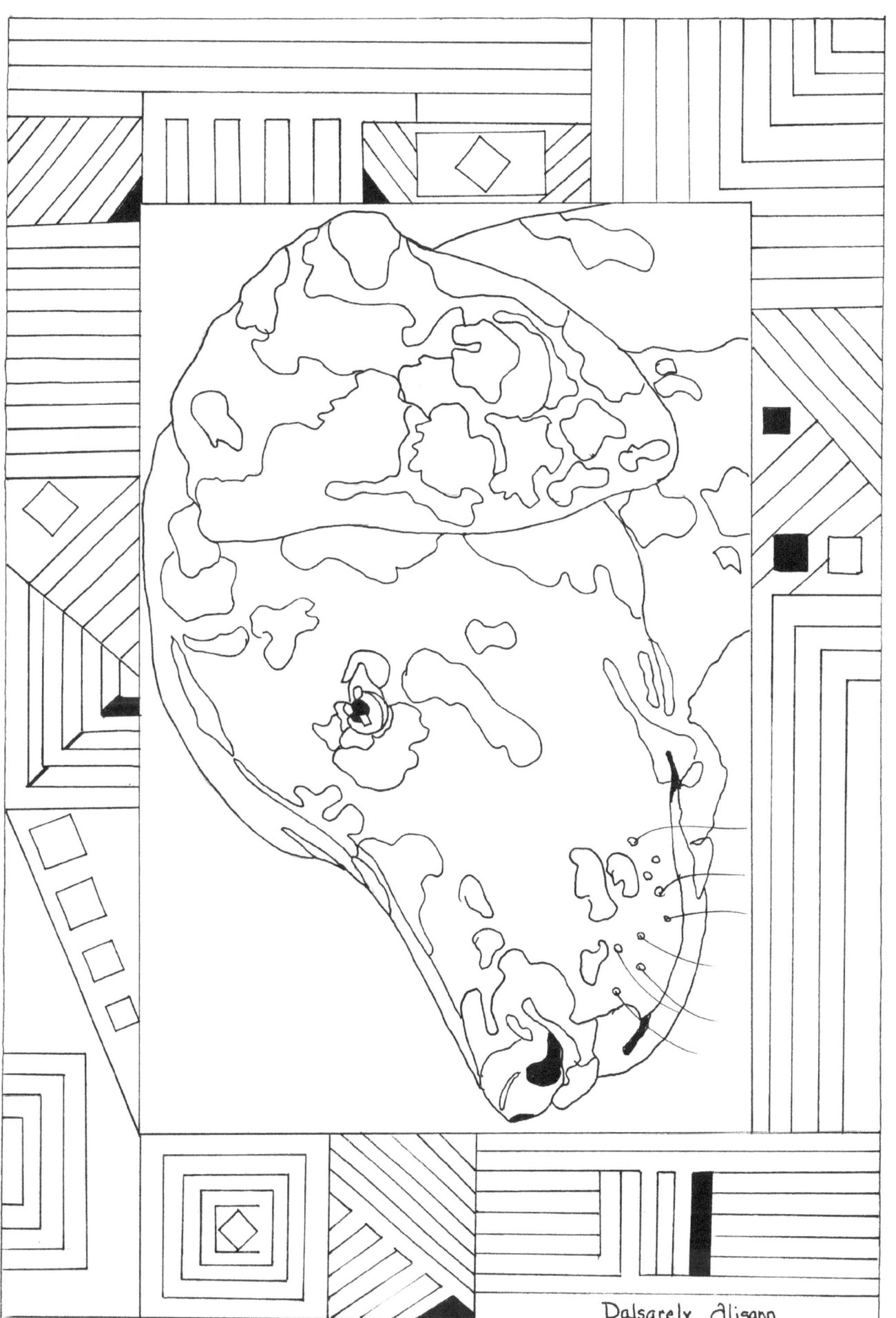

Dalsarely Alisann

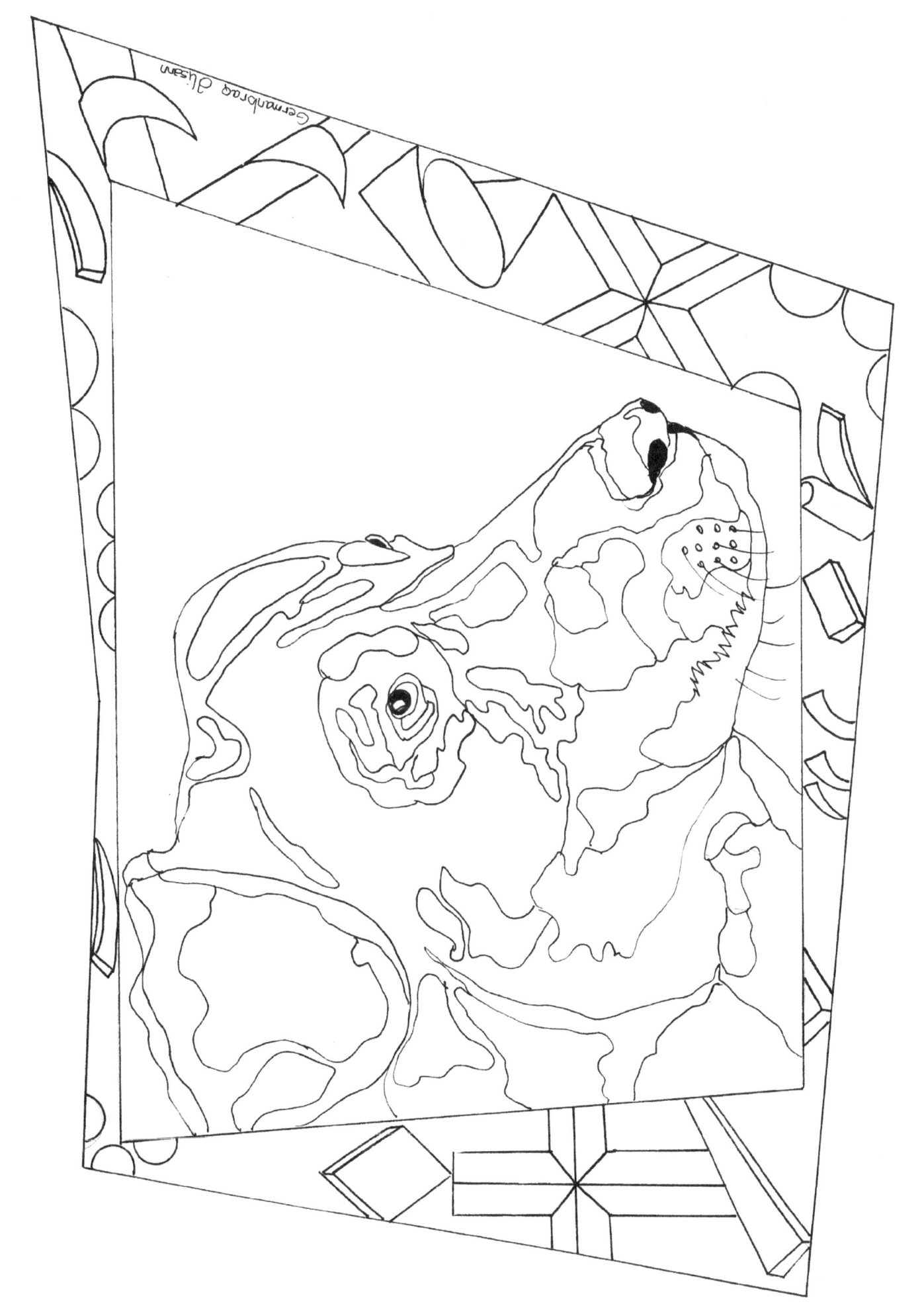

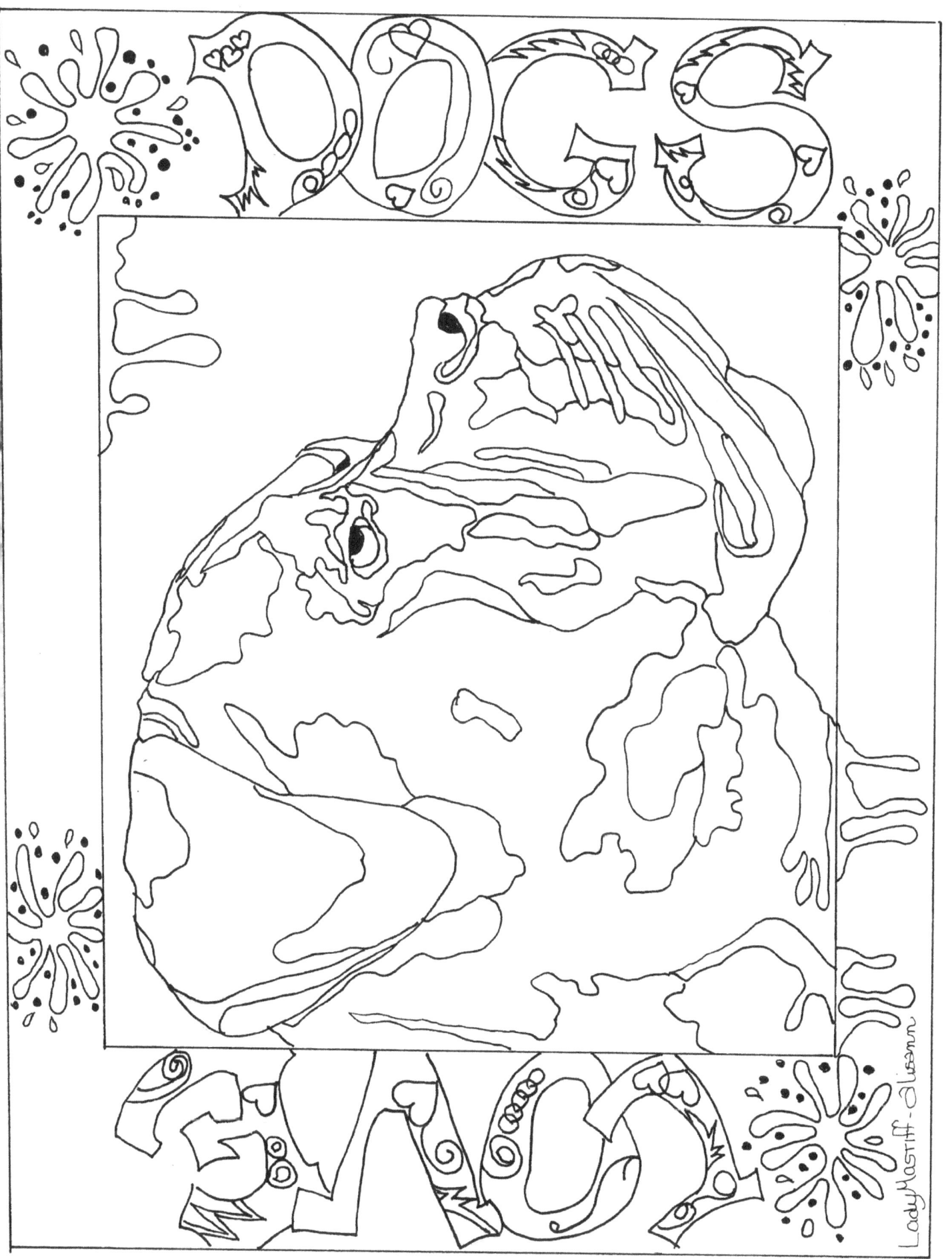

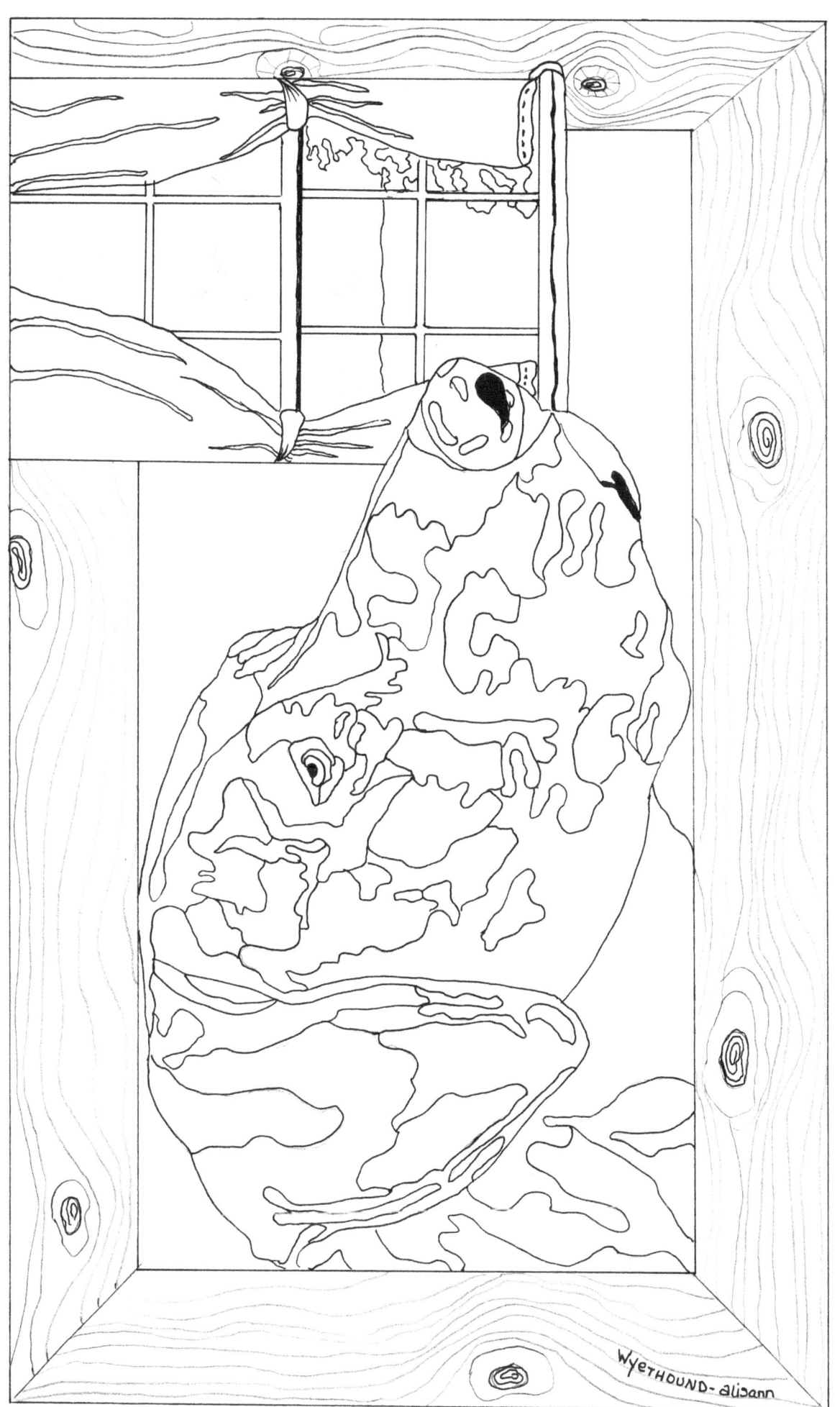

WYETHOUND-alisann

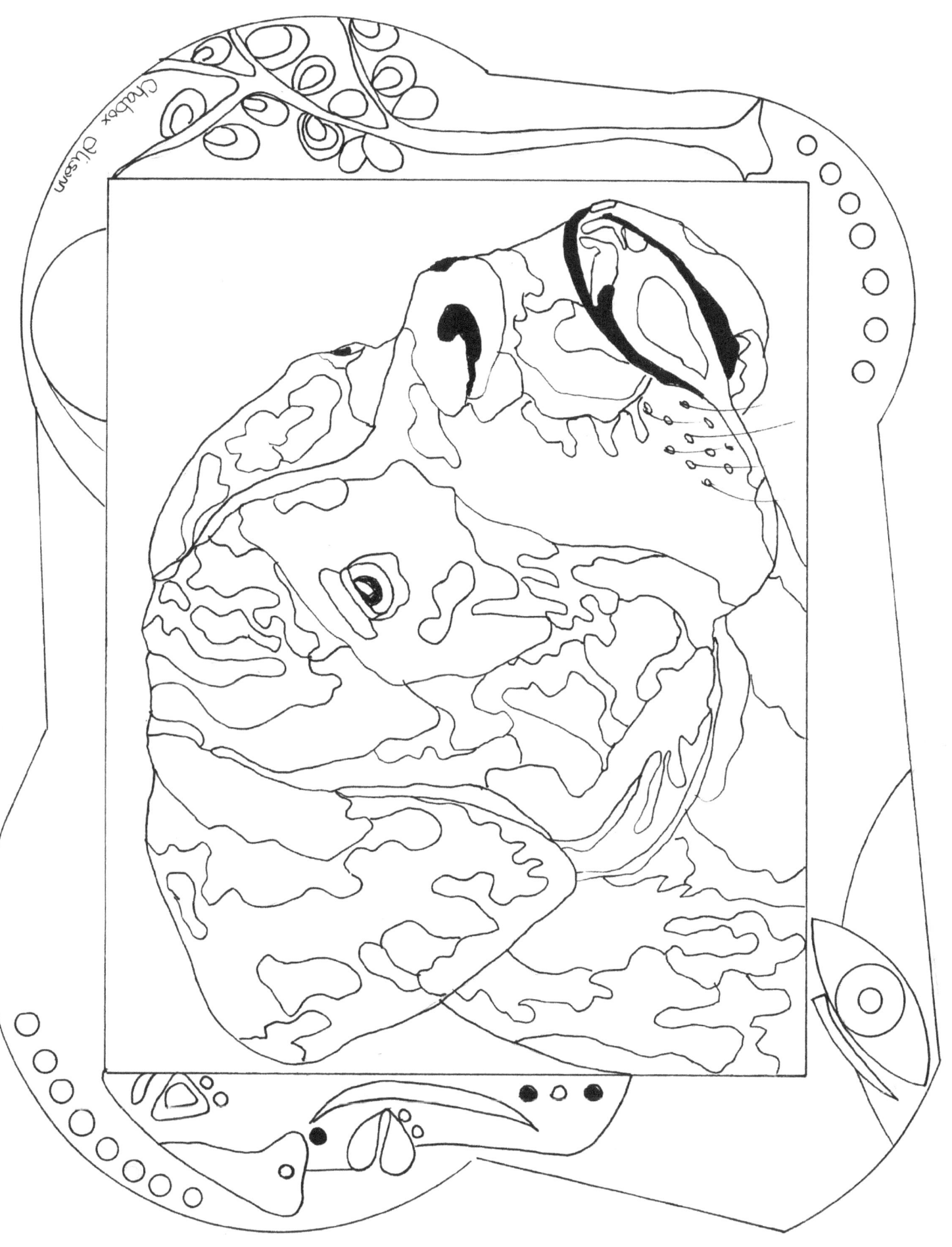

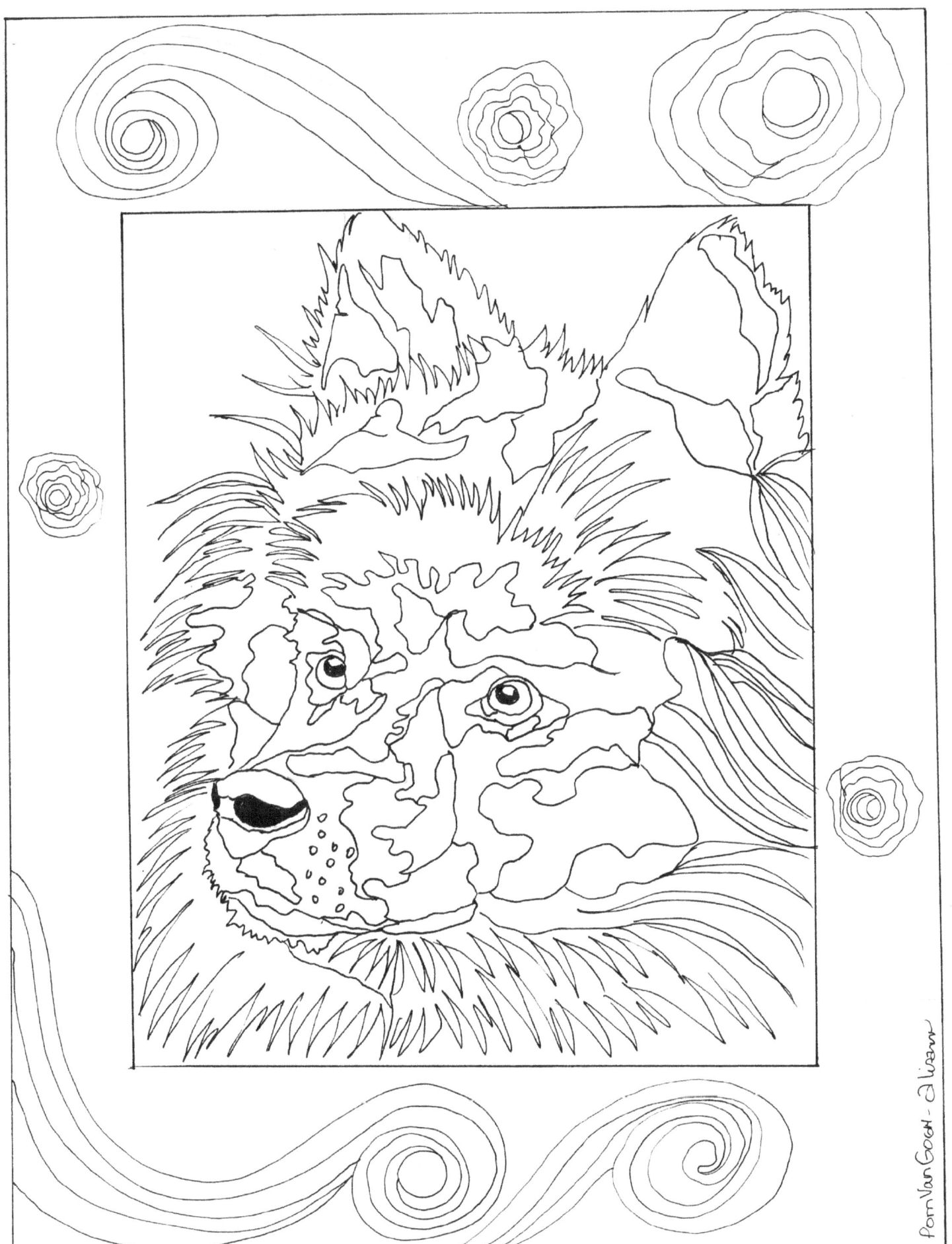

Pom Van Gogh - Alisson

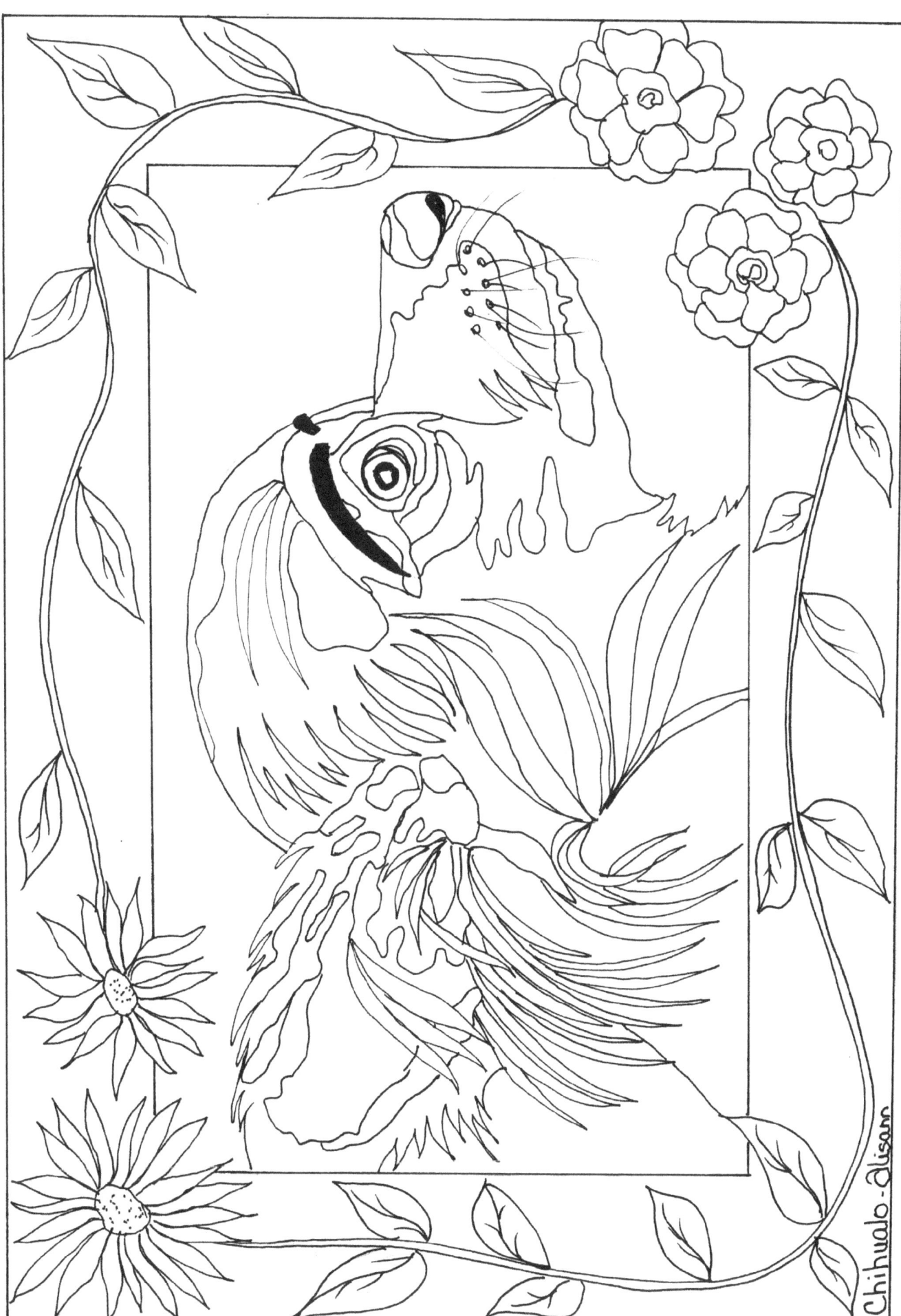
Chihuaha-Alisan

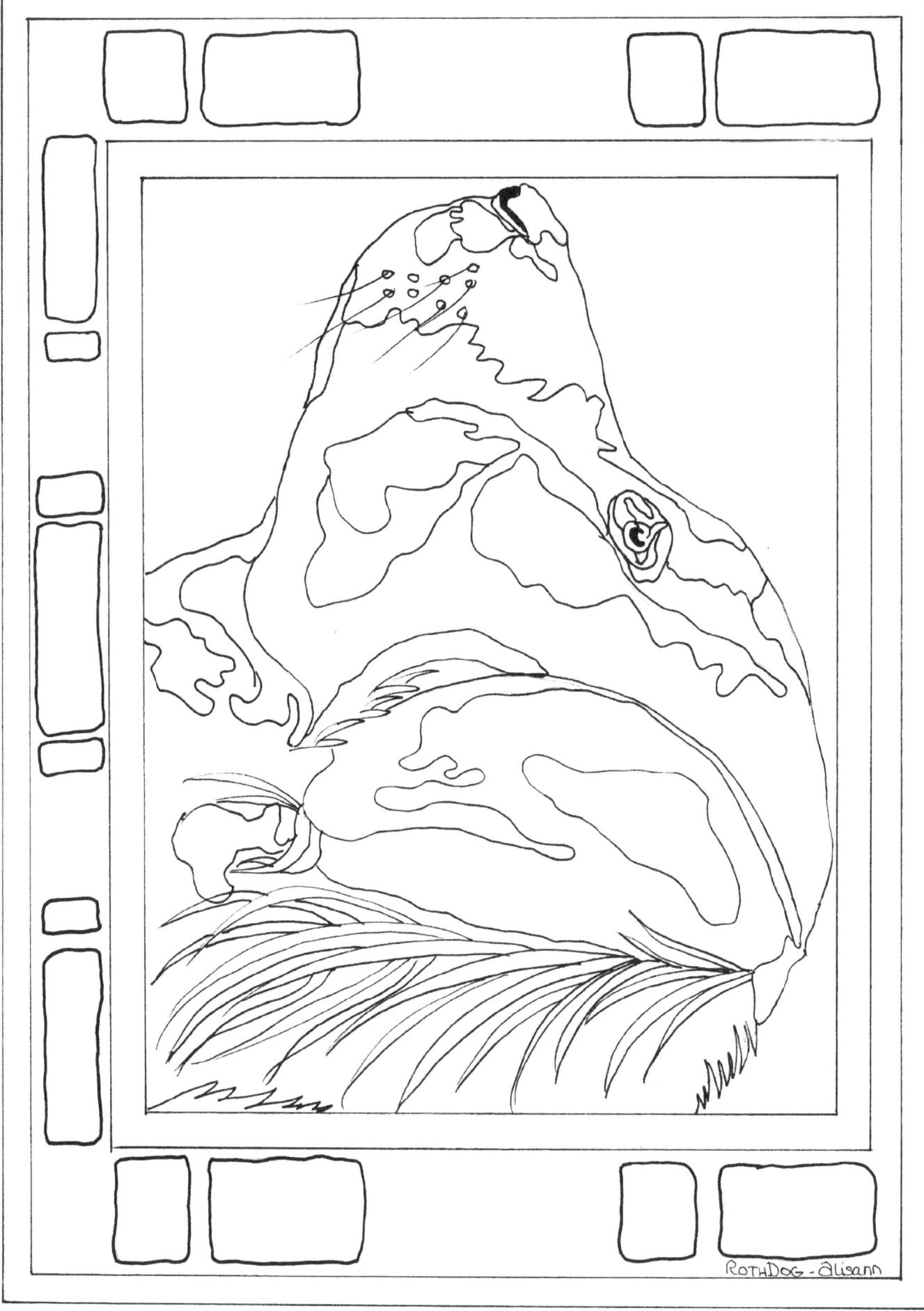

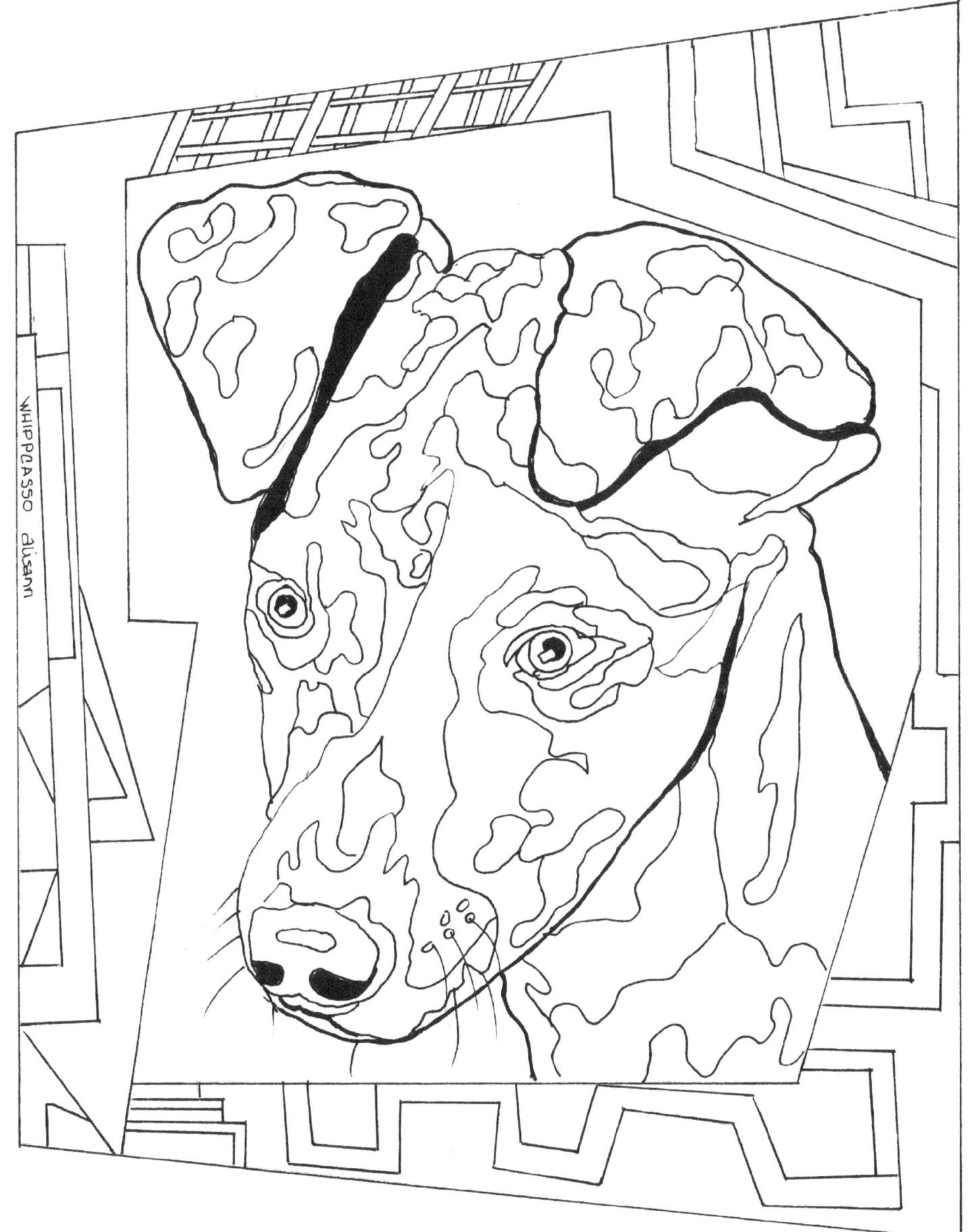

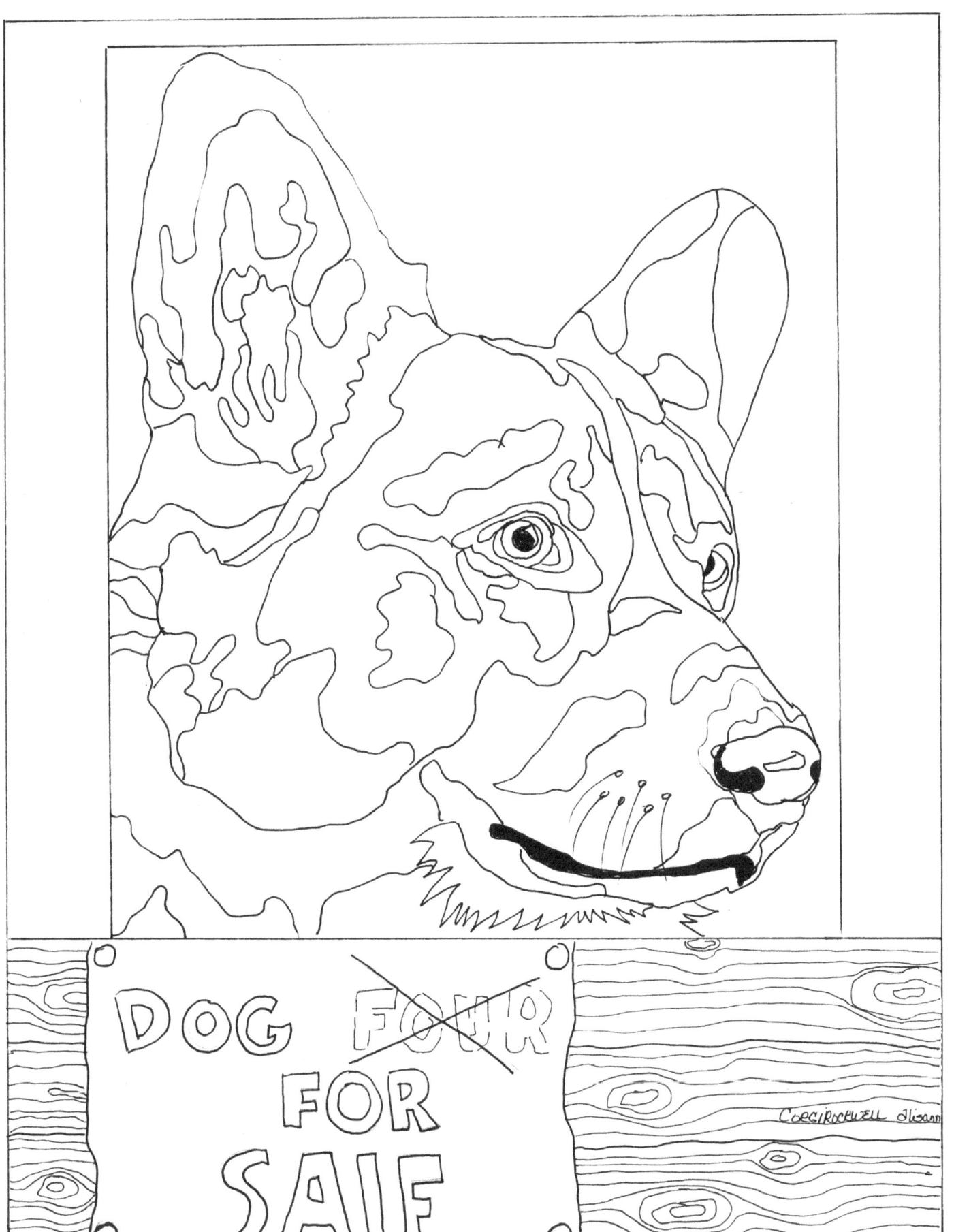

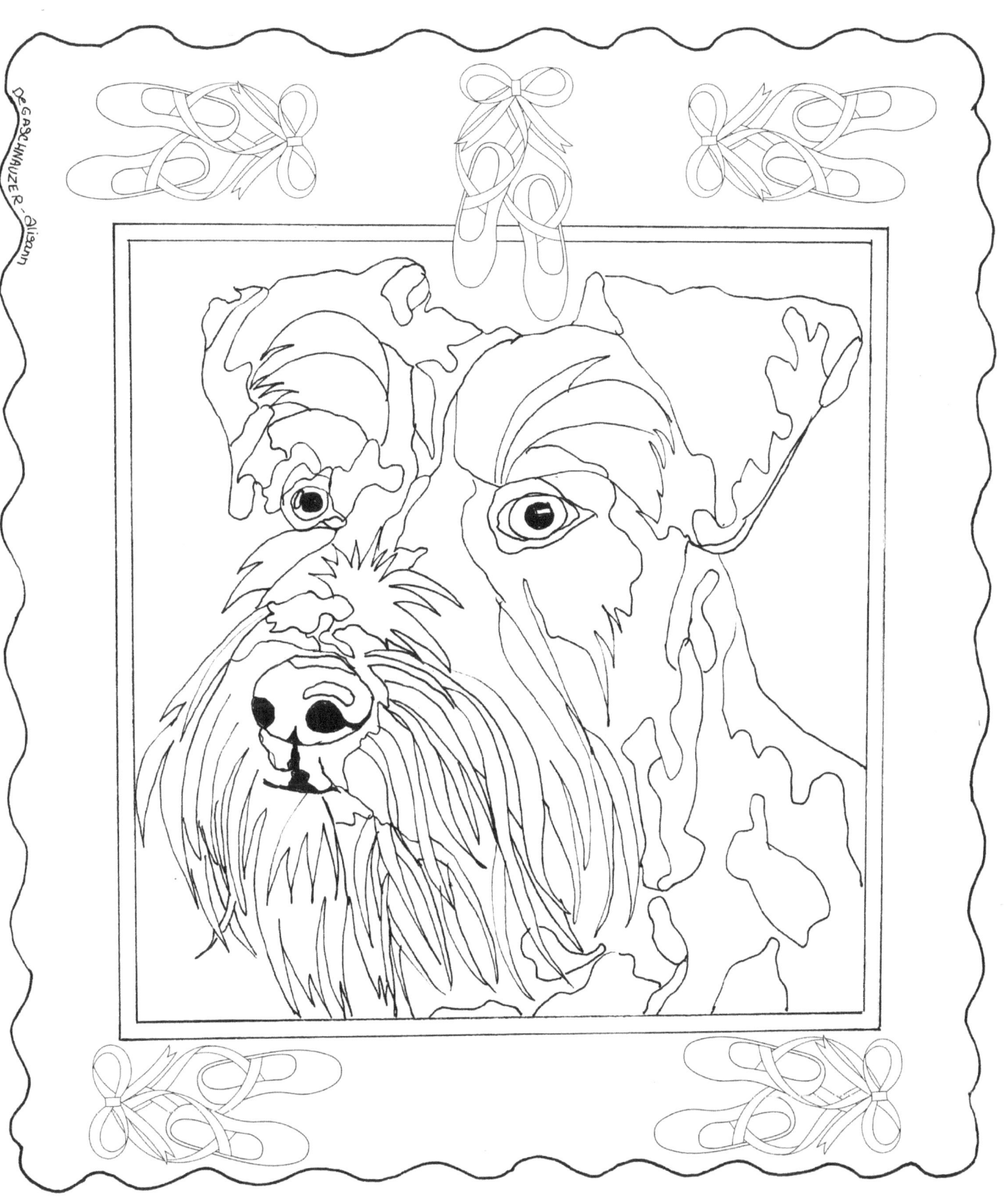

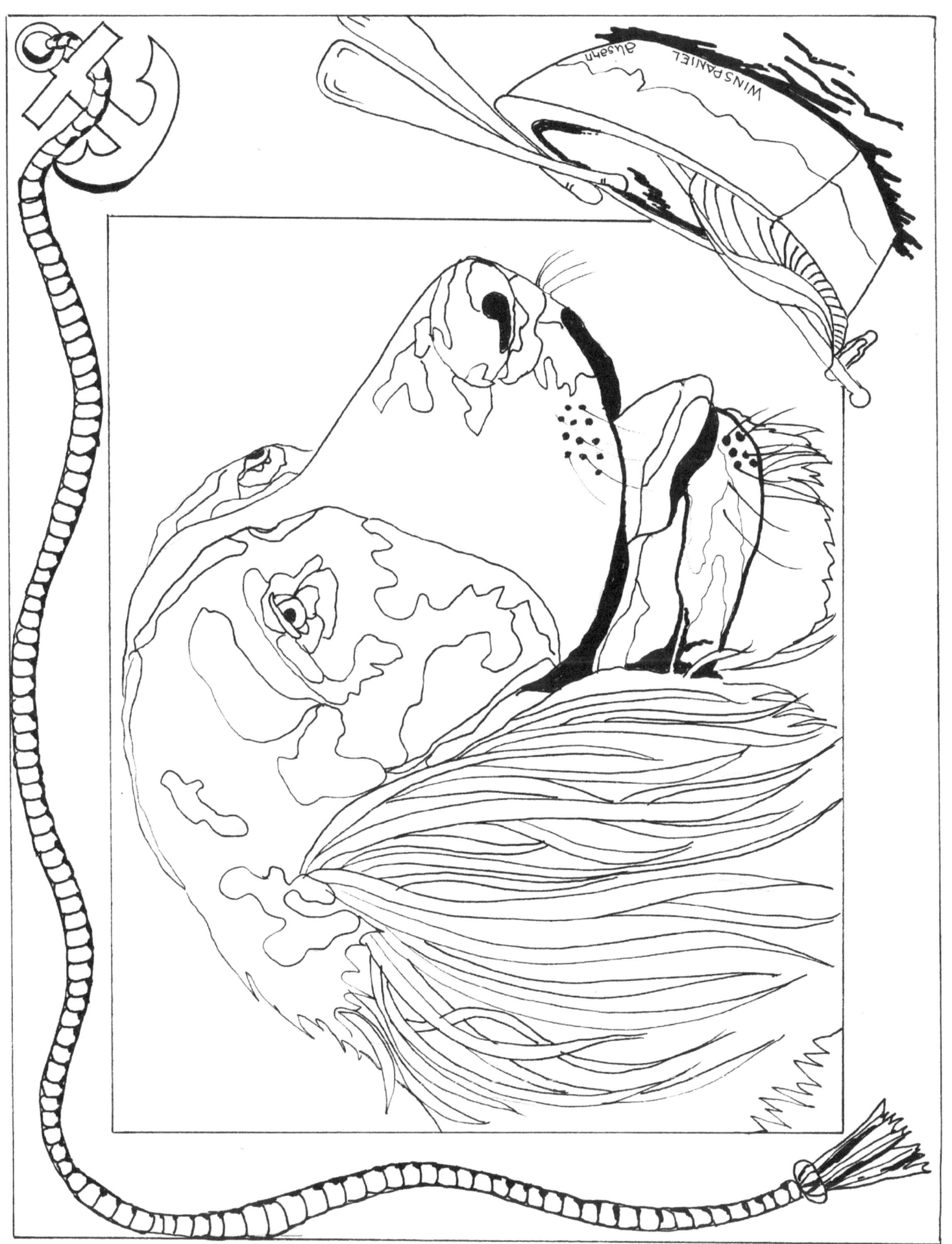

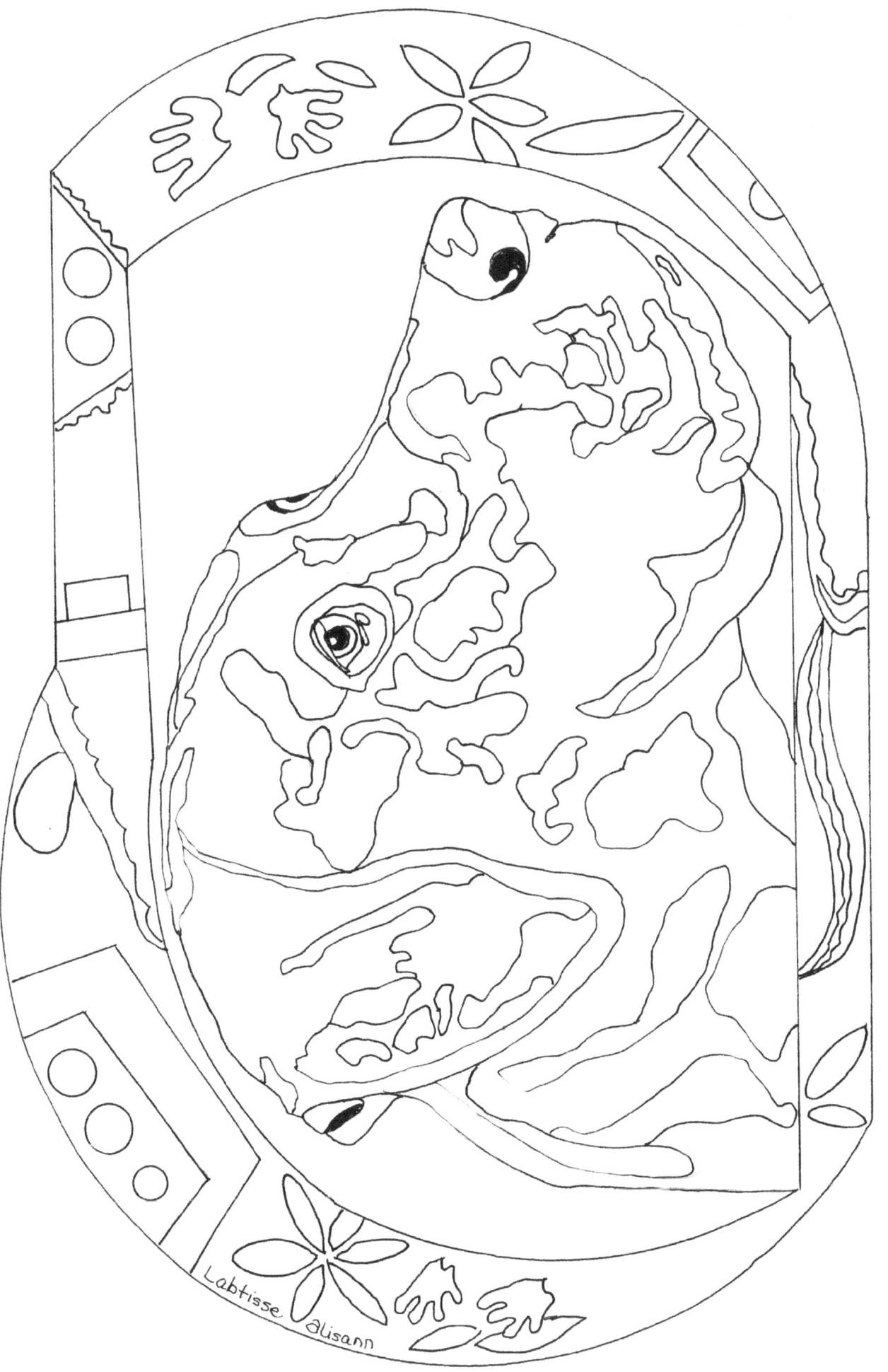

Labtisse Alisann

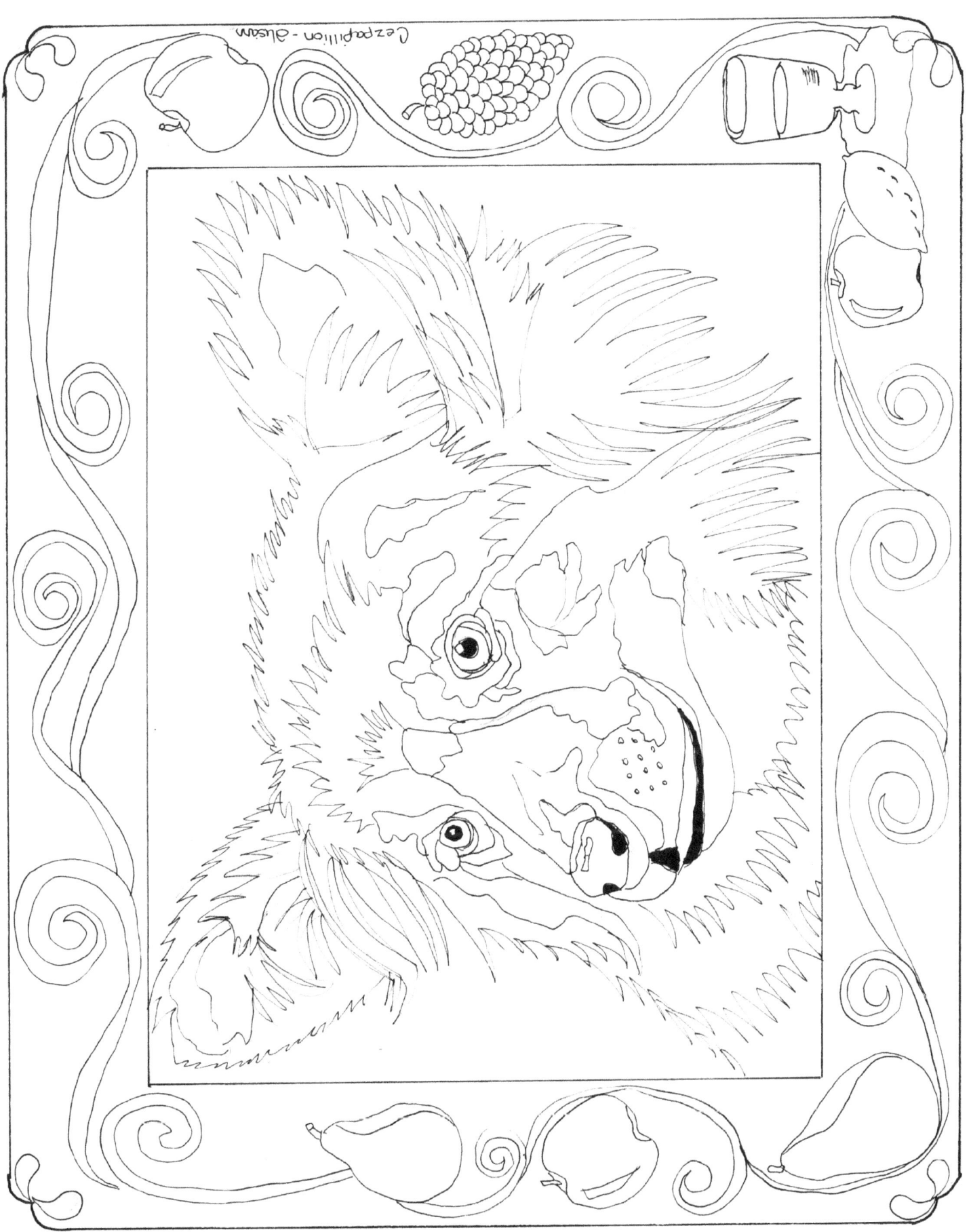

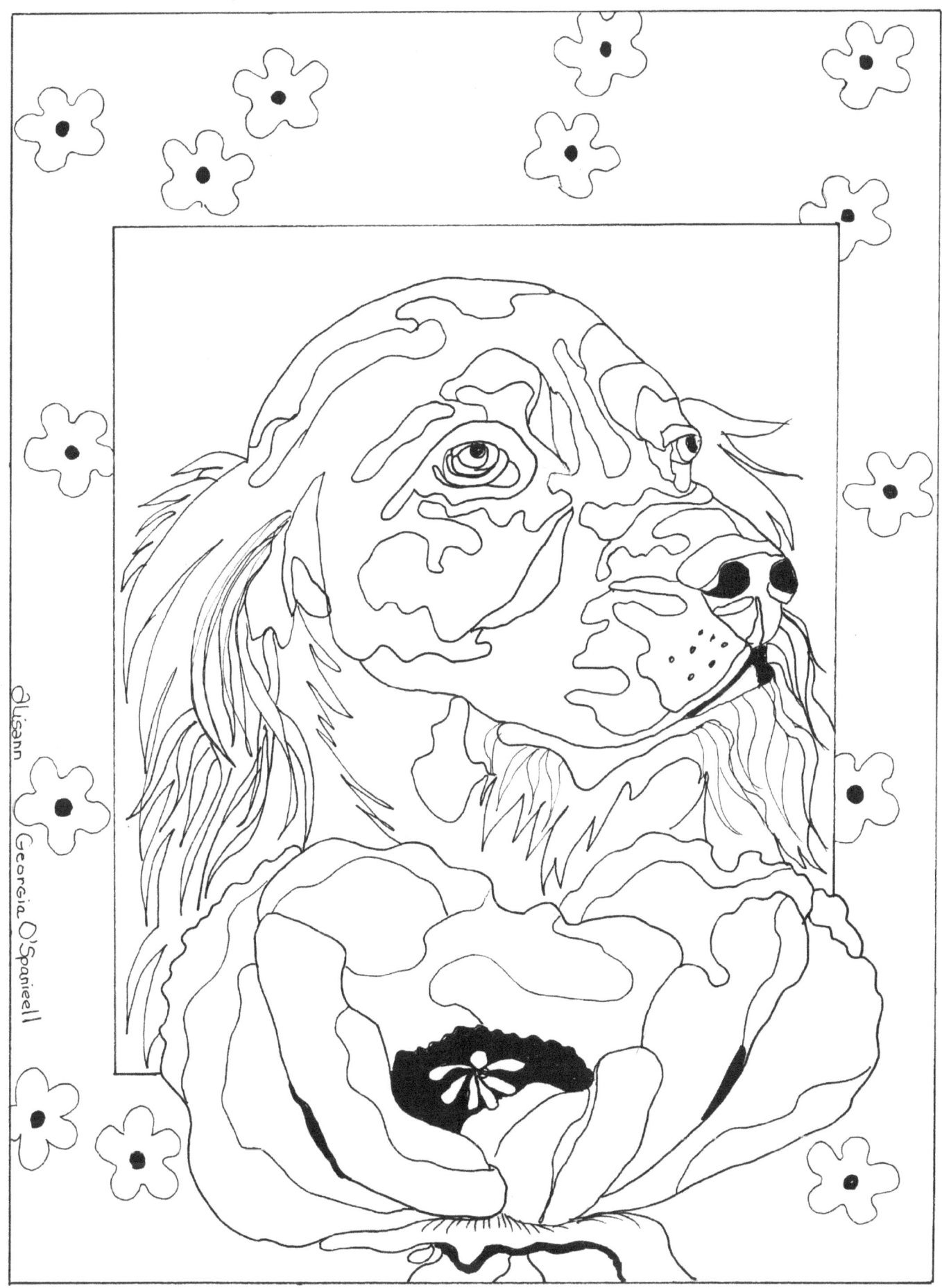

Lisann Georgia O'Spanieell

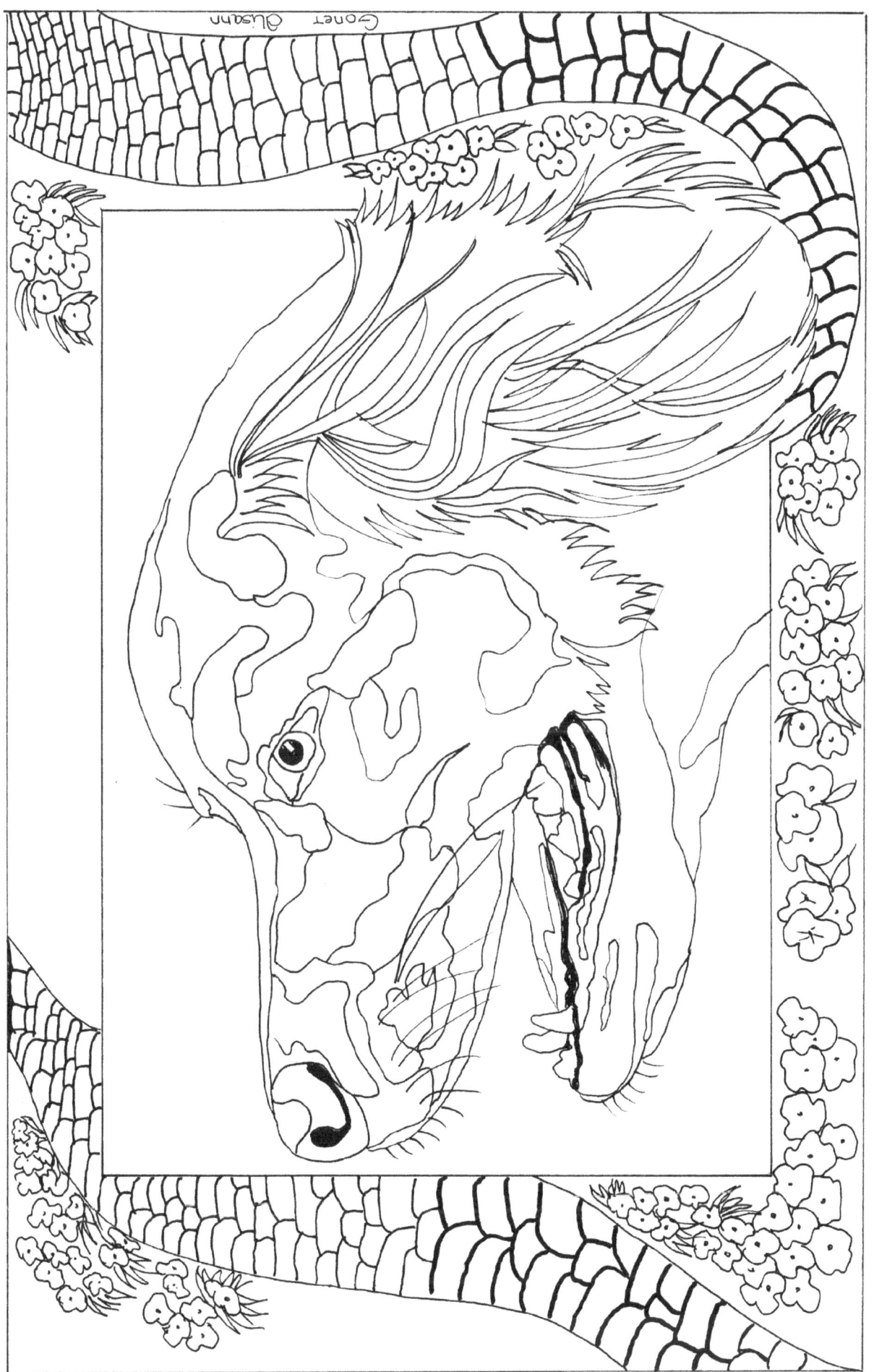

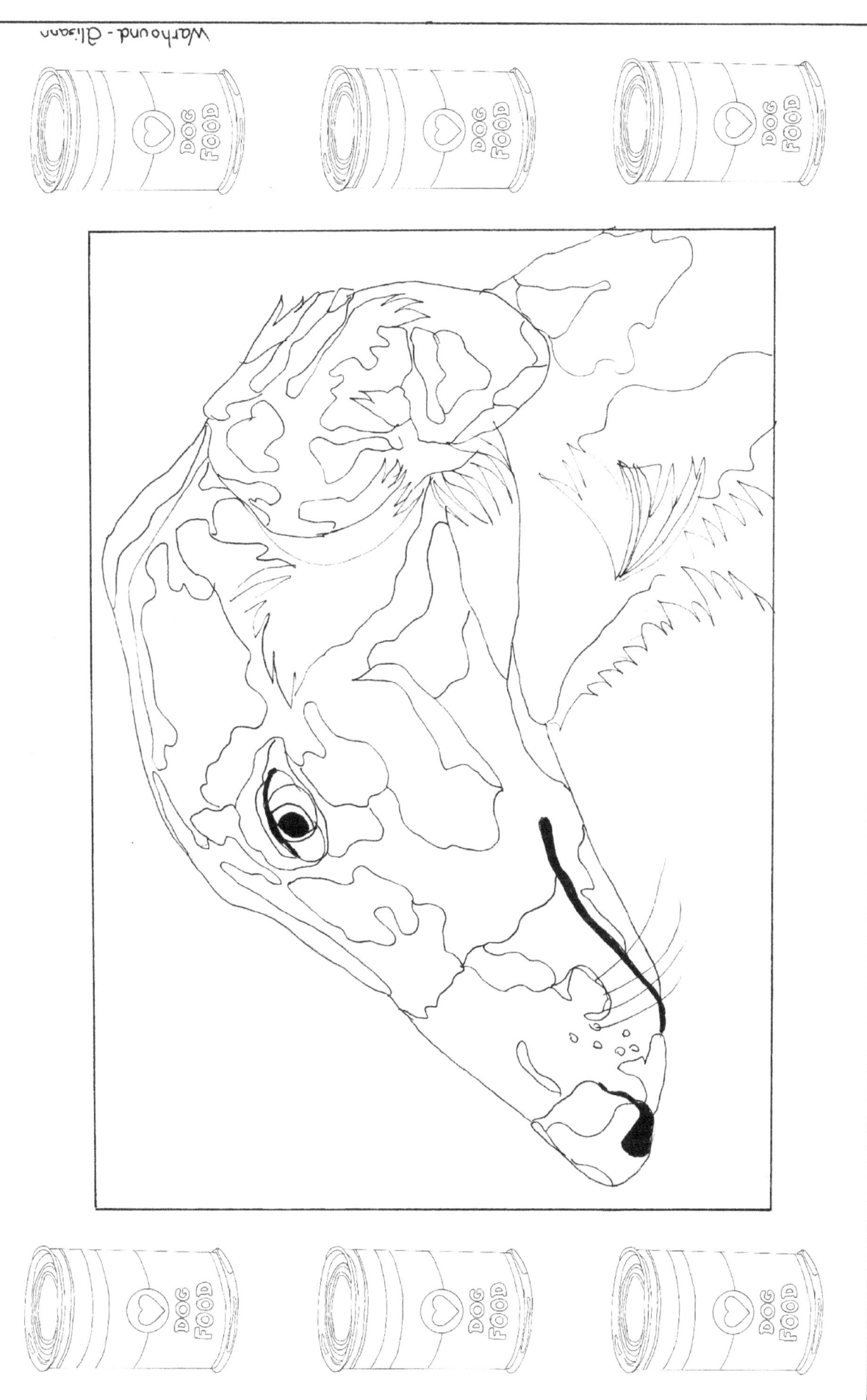

Warhound - Alisann

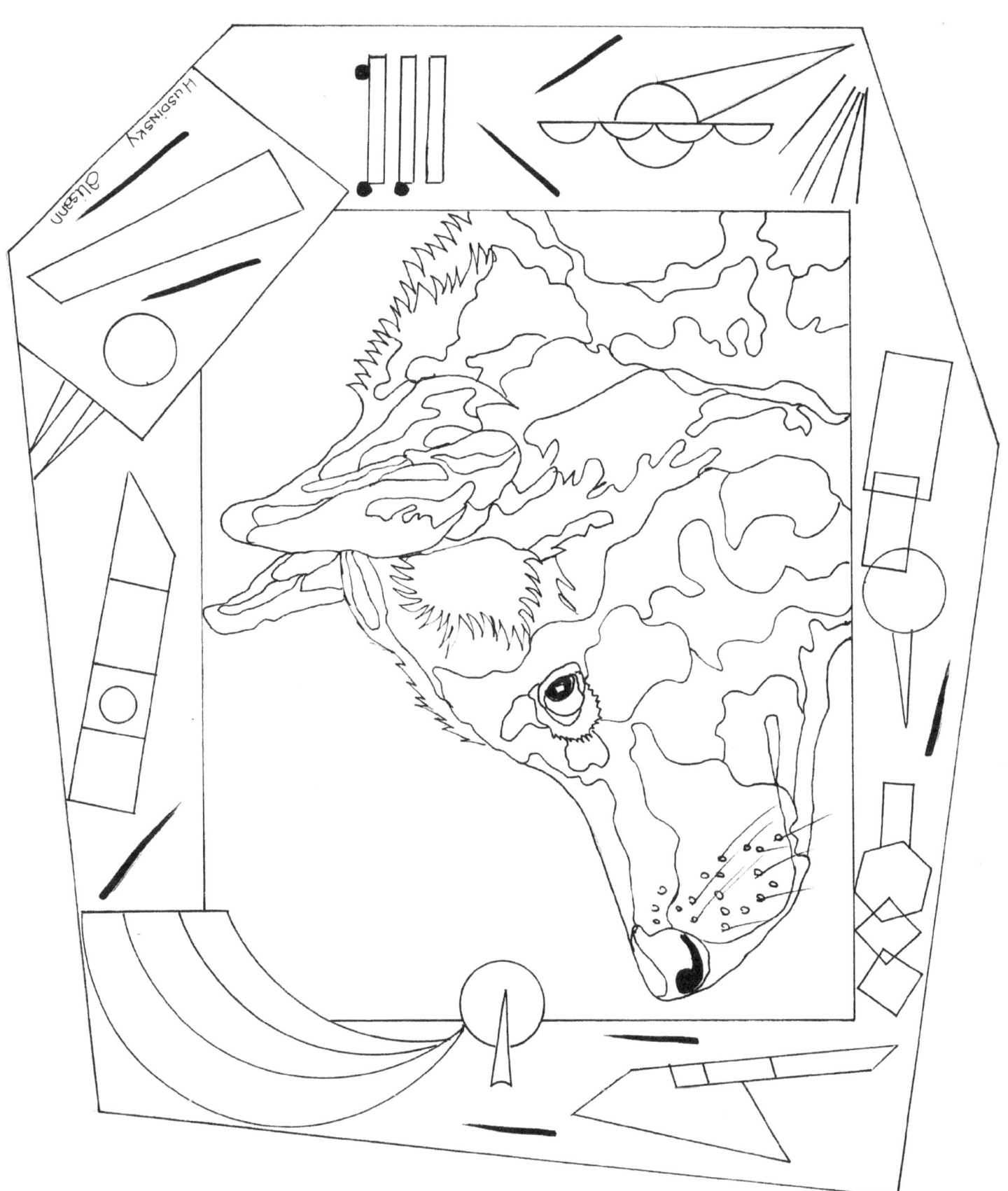

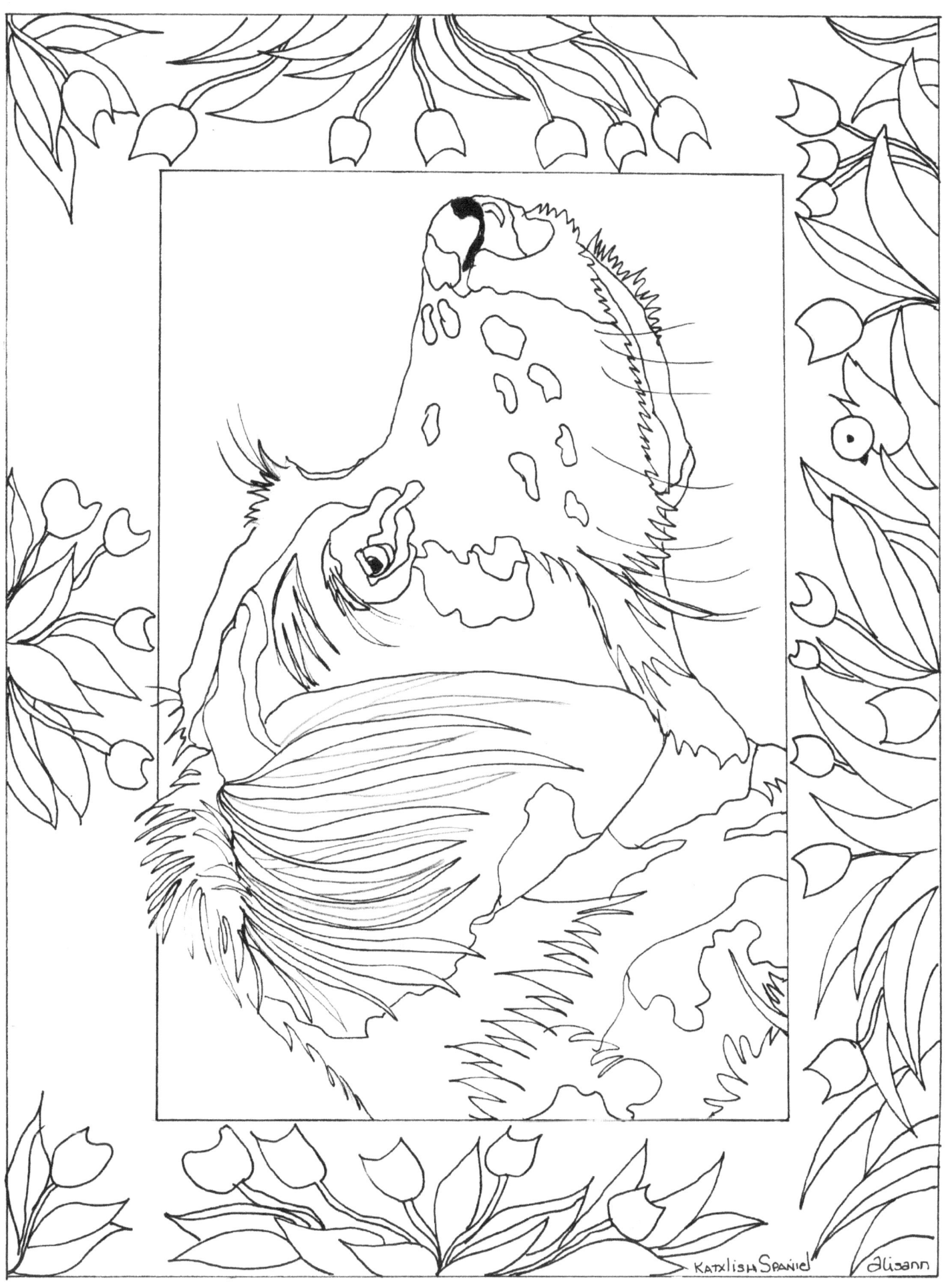

KatxlishSpaniel   alisann

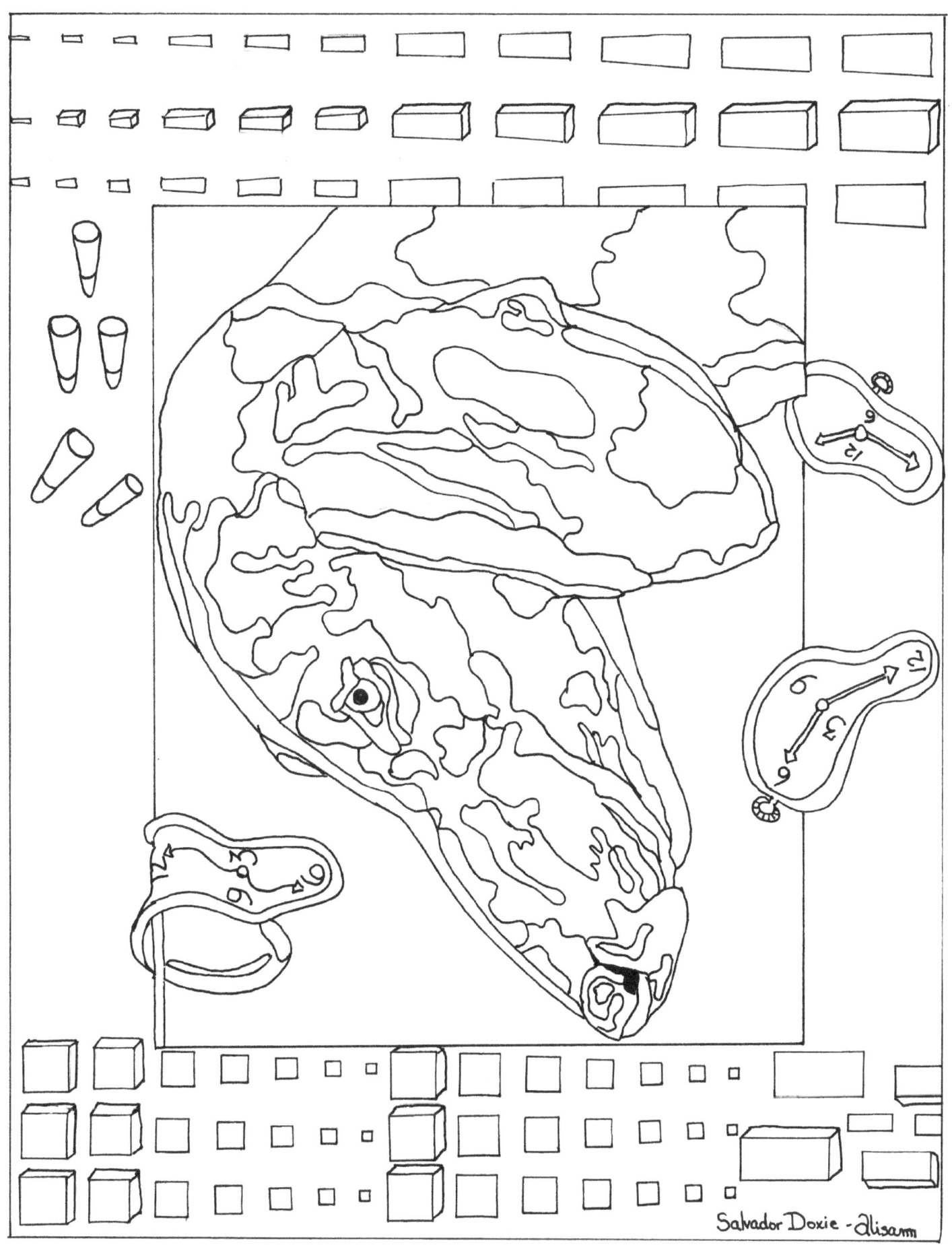

Salvador Doxie - Alisann

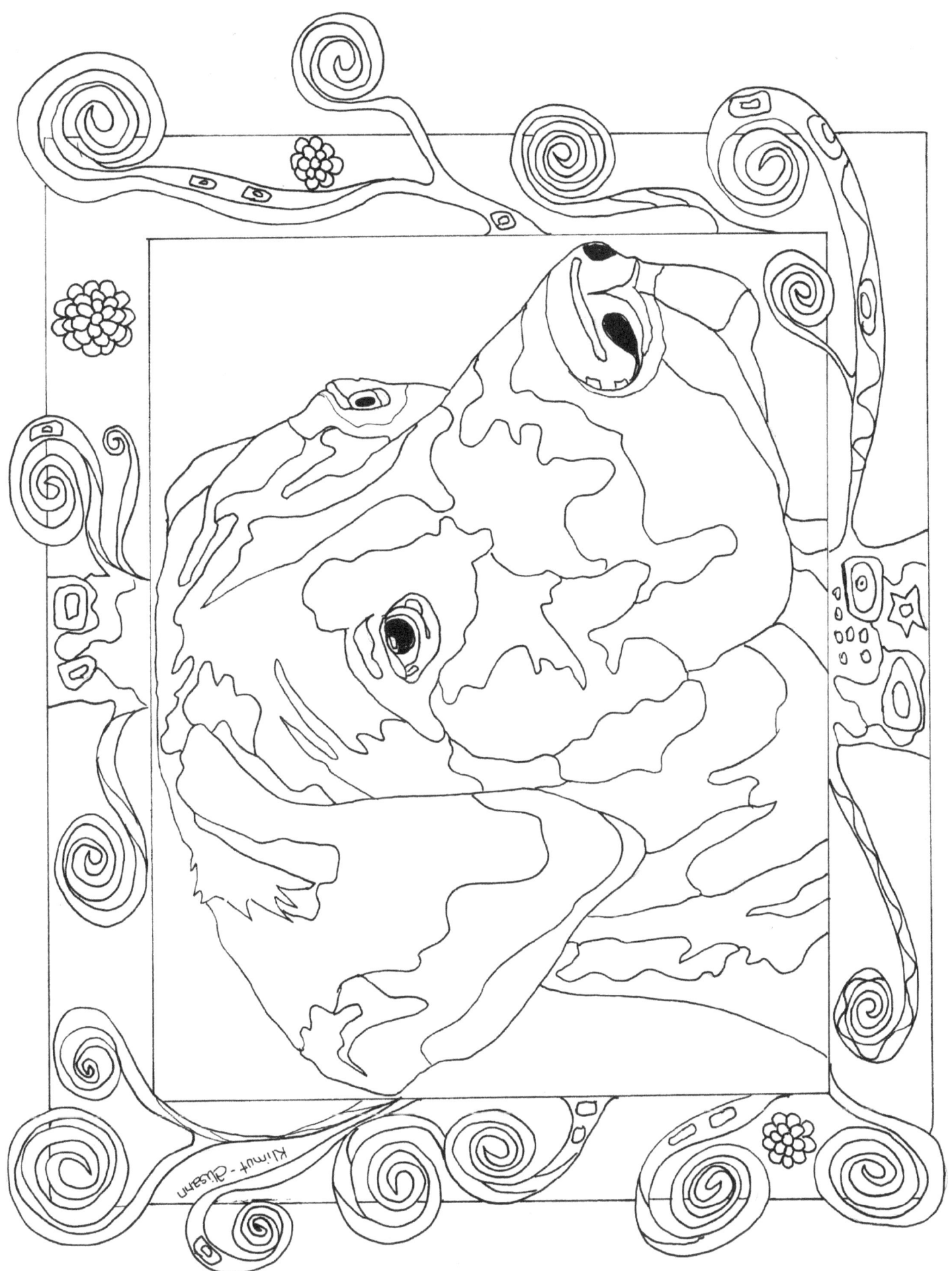

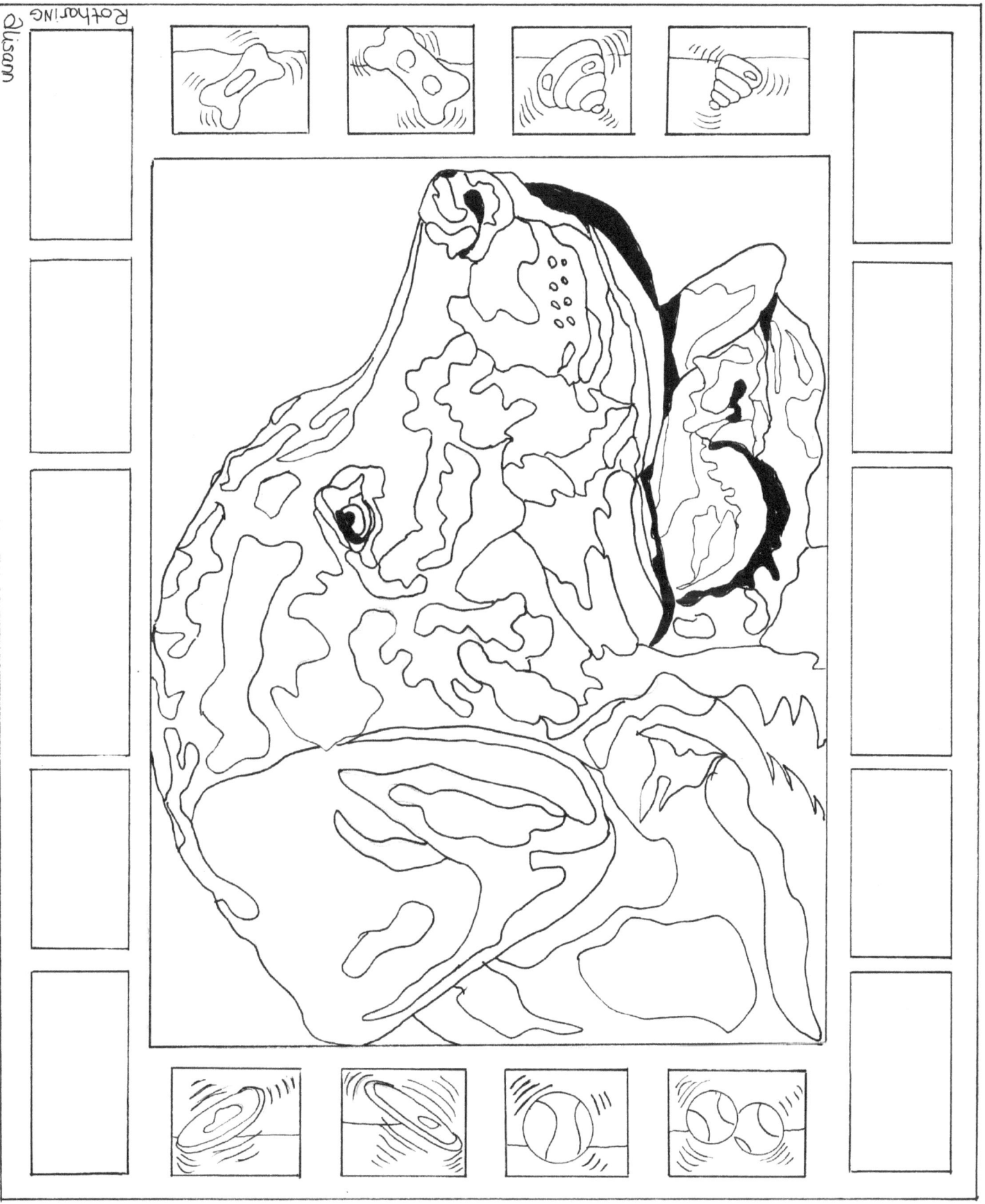

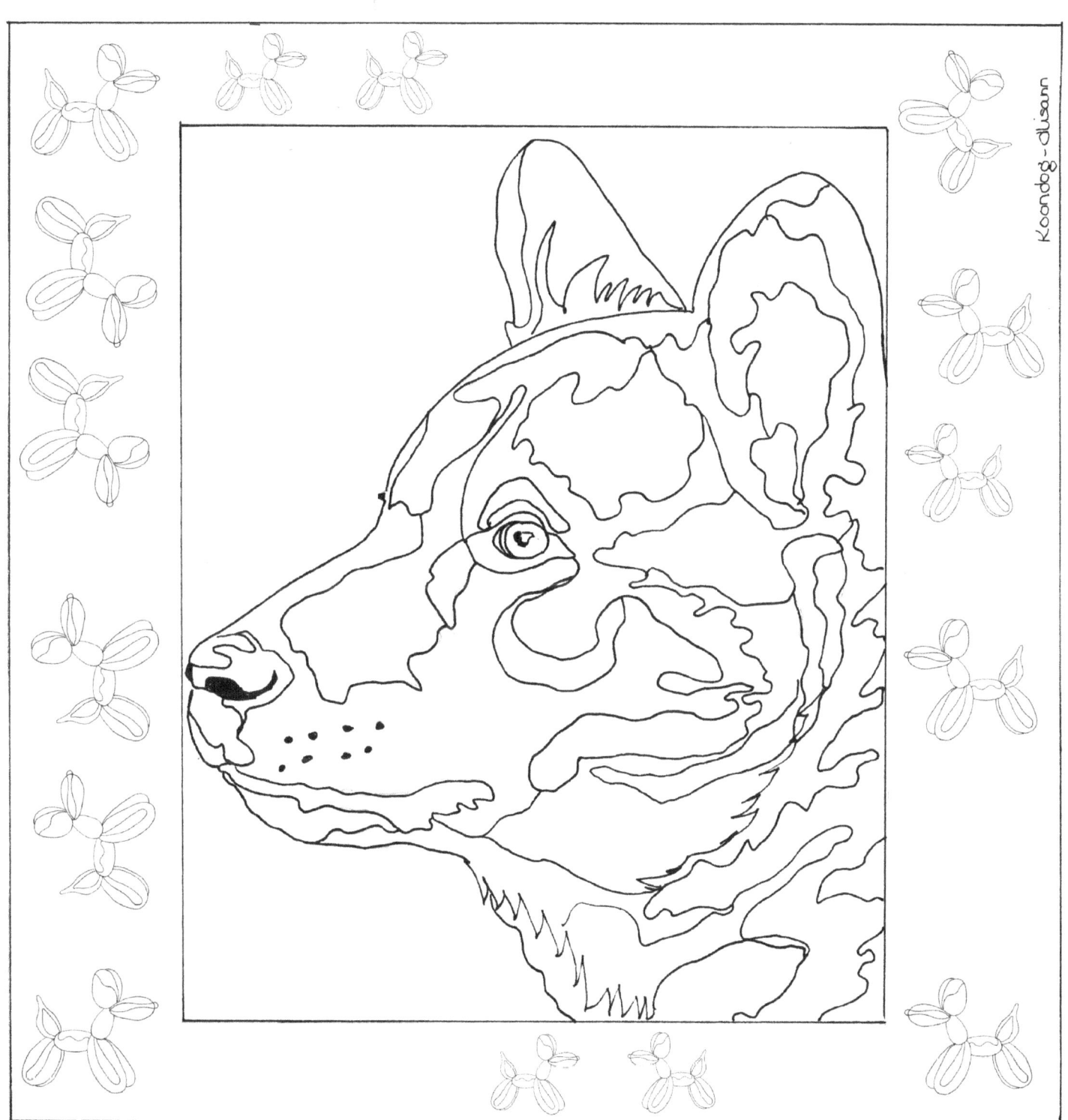

Koondog - dusann

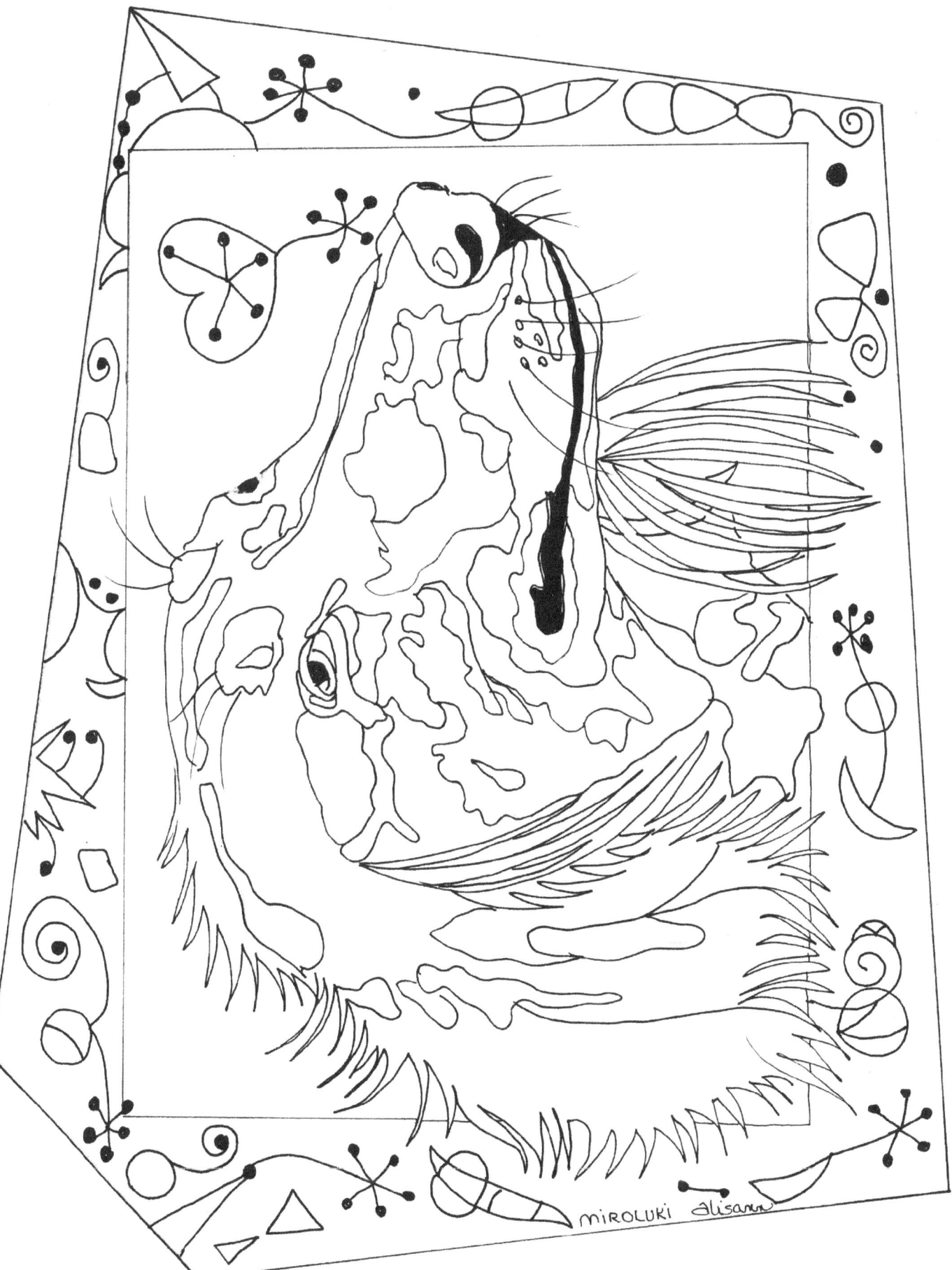

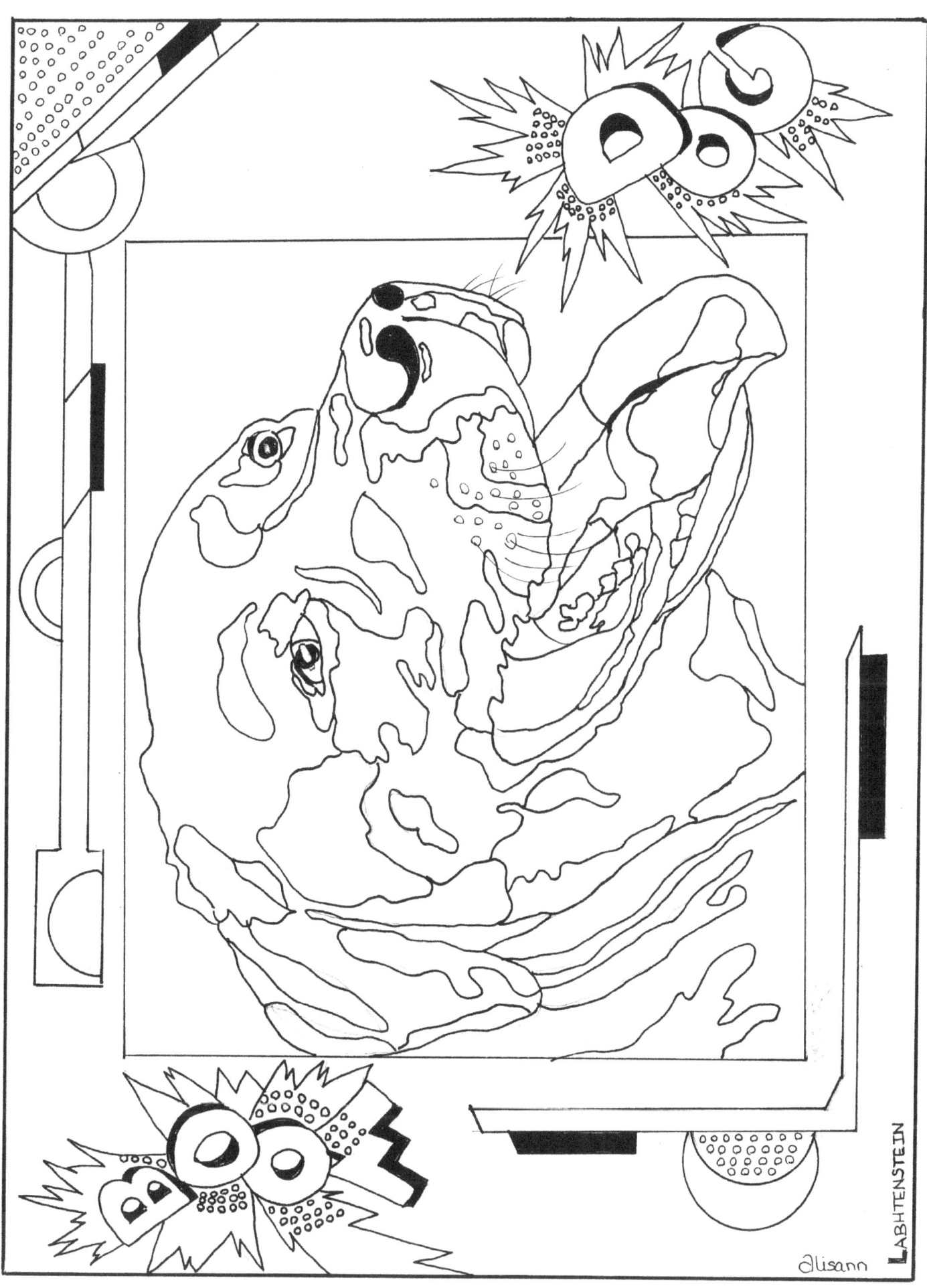

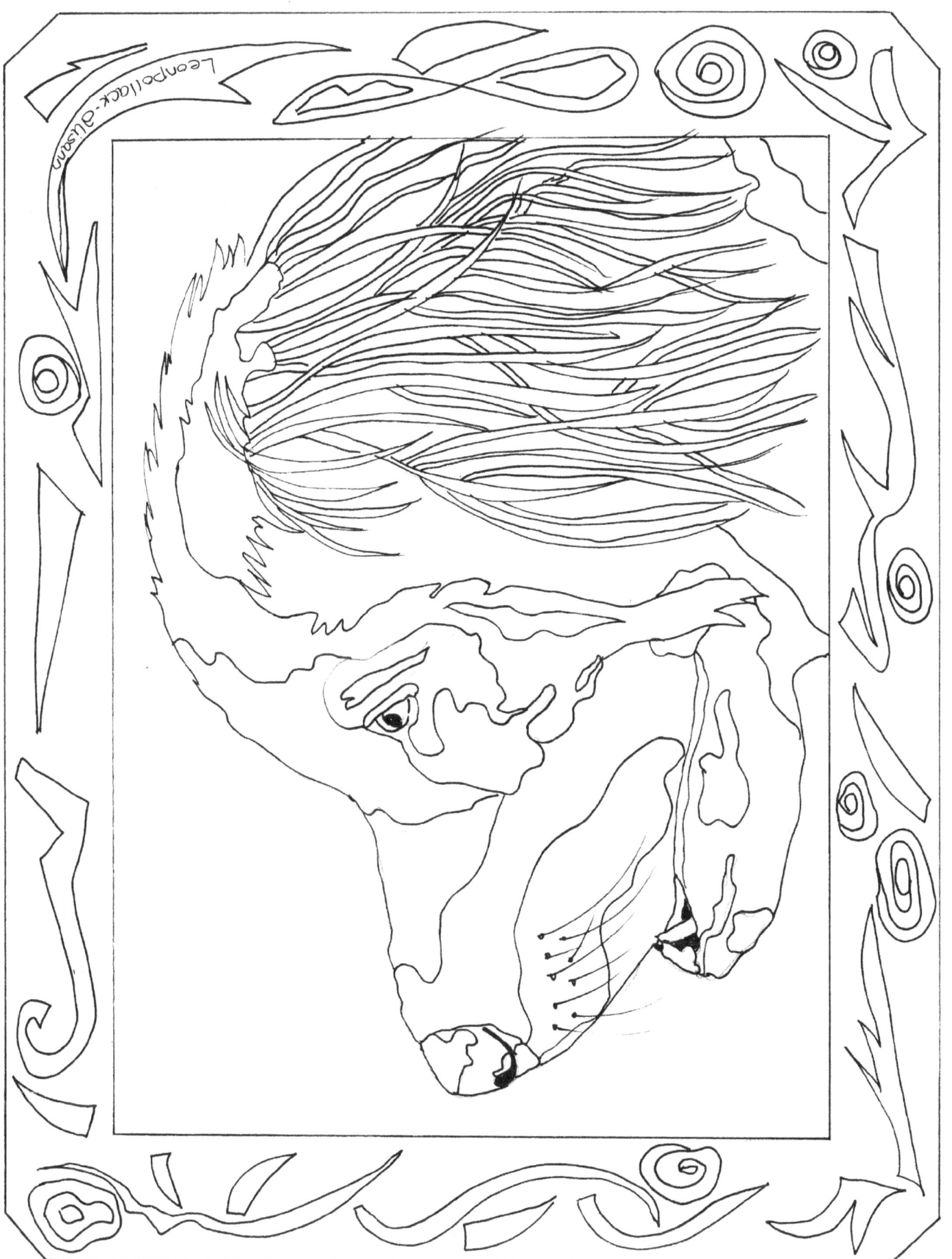

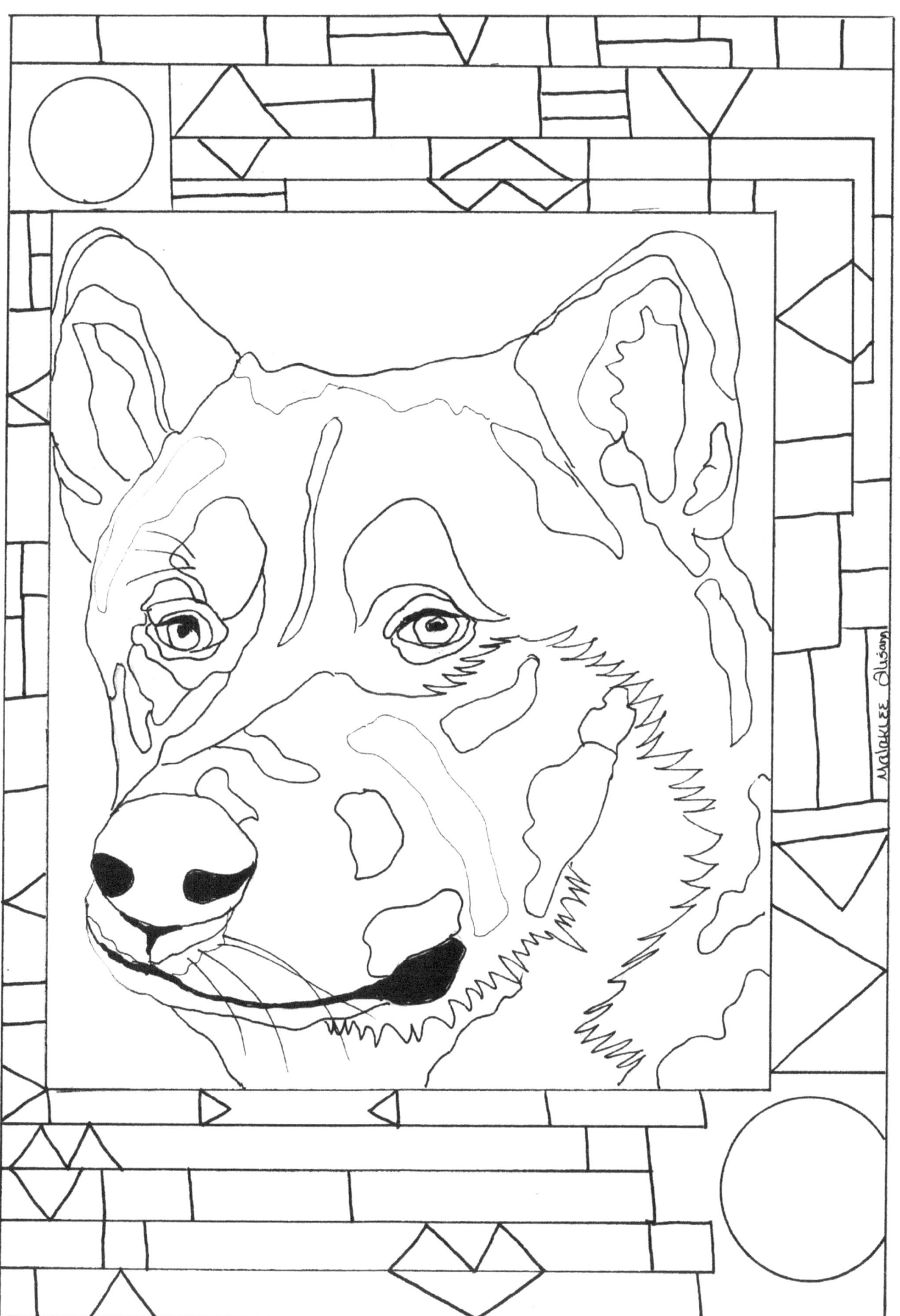

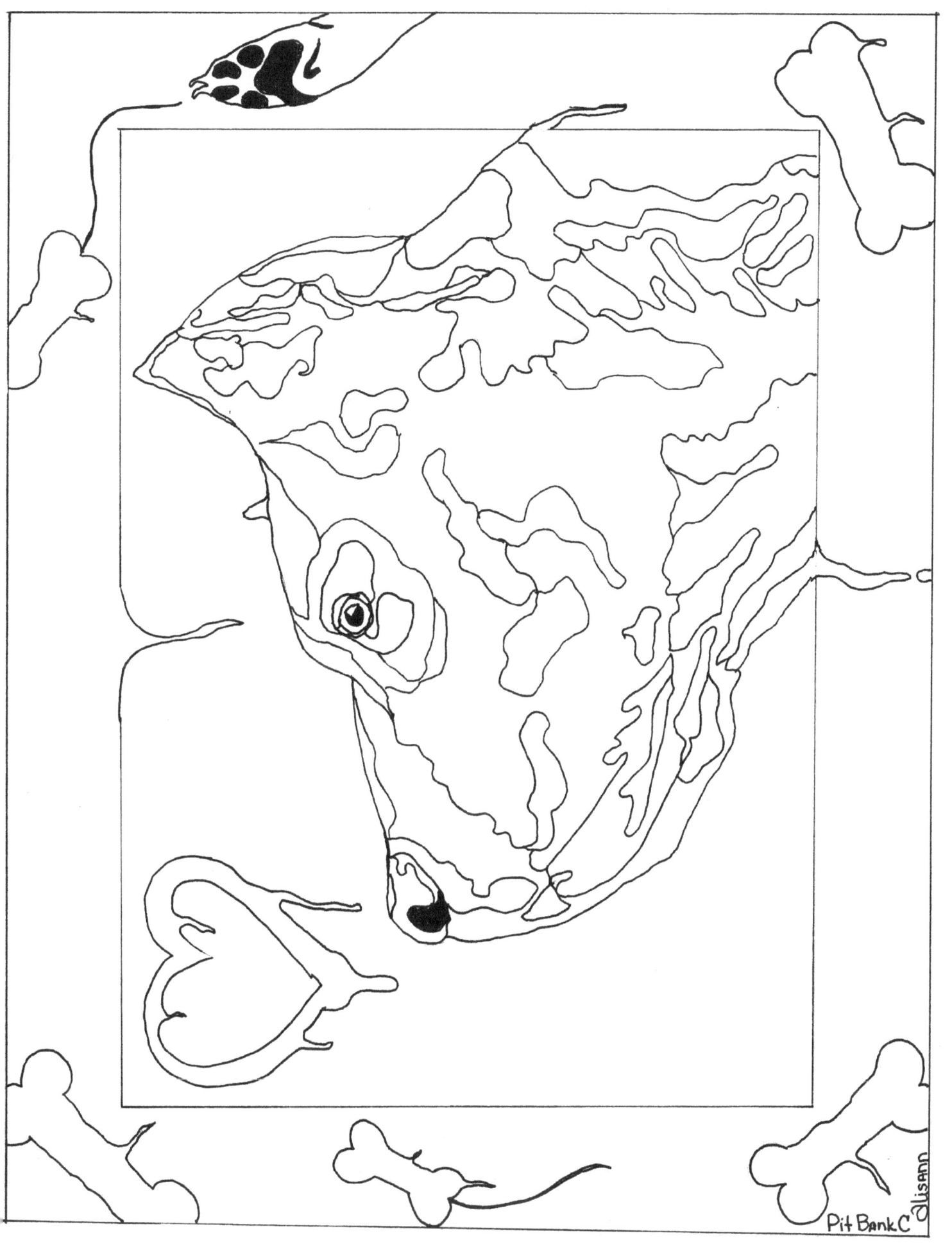

Pit Bank.C Alisann

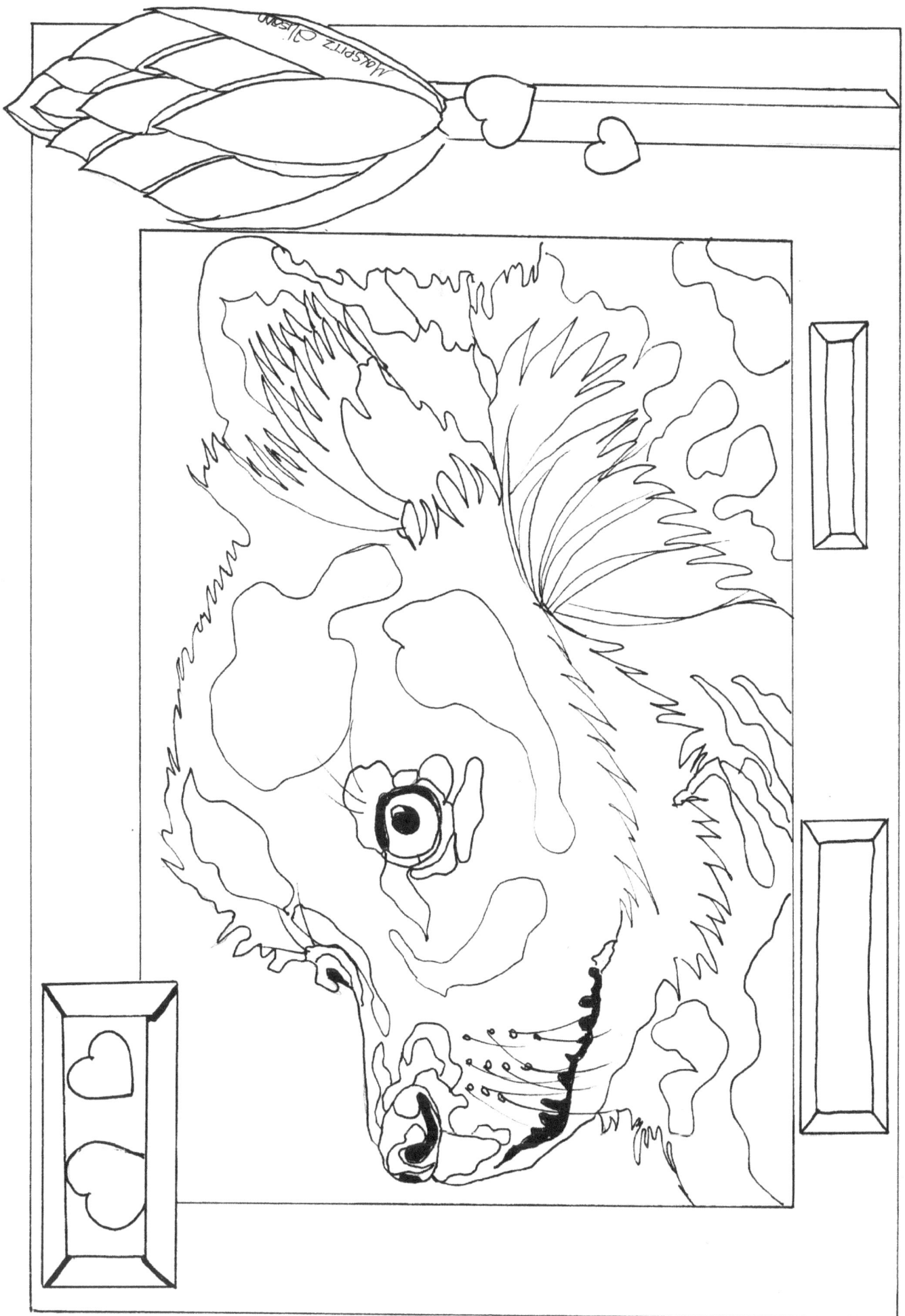